Beyond Memory

SUNY series in Italian/American Culture
―――――――
Fred L. Gardaphe, editor

Beyond Memory

Italian Protestants in Italy and America

Dennis Barone

Published by State University of New York Press, Albany

© 2016 State University of New York

All rights reserved

Printed in the United States of America

No part of this book may be used or reproduced in any manner whatsoever without written permission. No part of this book may be stored in a retrieval system or transmitted in any form or by any means including electronic, electrostatic, magnetic tape, mechanical, photocopying, recording, or otherwise without the prior permission in writing of the publisher.

For information, contact State University of New York Press, Albany, NY
www.sunypress.edu

Production, Emily Keneston
Marketing, Anne M. Valentine

Library of Congress Cataloging-in-Publication Data

Names: Barone, Dennis, author.
Title: Beyond memory : Italian protestants in Italy and America / Dennis Barone.
Description: Albany, NY : State University of New York Press, 2016. | Series: SUNY series in Italian/American culture | Includes bibliographical references and index.
Identifiers: LCCN 2016005976 | ISBN 9781438462158 (hardcover : alk. paper) | ISBN 9781438462172 (e-book)
Subjects: LCSH: Italian American Protestants—History. | Italian American Protestants—Social conditions. | Protestants—Italy—History.
Classification: LCC BR563.I8 B37 2016 | DDC 280/.408951073—dc23
LC record available at https://lccn.loc.gov/2016005976

10 9 8 7 6 5 4 3 2 1

Dedicated to
Michelle Heinzinger and Darlene Lipp
(le mie sorelle)

Contents

Introduction	1
Chapter 1. The Soul of a Stranger	17
Chapter 2. To Struggle for a Place at the Table	37
Chapter 3. Does Christ Linger at Eboli?	49
Chapter 4. Answers to the Roman Question	67

photo gallery follows page 84

Chapter 5. By Twos and by Threes	85
Chapter 6. Christ for Hartford	99
Chapter 7. A Sermon for the Oppressed	113
Epilogue	141
Works Cited	155
Index	167

Introduction

Early Sunday morning my wife and I had attended services at the Chiesa Valdese on the Piazza Cavour. Unfortunately, the facade had been wrapped in scaffolding for a restoration project. But the Valdese take their motto from the start of the gospel of John: "The light shines in the darkness, and the darkness has not overcome it."

It's not what people think about when they think about Rome. A pilgrimage to Rome usually centers on a blessing from the Pope in Saint Peter's Square. We had come to Rome—my wife and I—so that I could speak about the evangelization efforts of Rev. Alfredo Barone, in and around the southern Italian town of Calitri during the 1890s. I spoke at the historical conference "150 Years of Baptist Witness in Italy" (150 anni di testimoninza battista in Italia, 1863–2013), held at the Waldensian Faculty of Theology just around the corner from the Waldensain Church and the Piazza Cavour, an appropriate location since Count Cavour, a leader of the reunification of modern Italy, famously proclaimed, "A free church in a free state."

But there has been a conflicted relationship between church and state ever since the unification. Religious liberty has often been pledged, and yet even as recently as 2012 the Milan City Council closed evangelical churches and similar closures occurred throughout Lombardy. State schools must teach religion classes that are controlled by Catholic Church authorities, something that would be hard to imagine in the United States.

Pastor Adamo at the Valdese Church on the Piazza Cavour had impressed me with his preaching ex tempore, without notes and rich in gesture. The organ-backed hymns could have easily been mistaken for the Sunday singing of a Presbyterian congregation in New Jersey. When we arrived Pastor Adamo conducted a young couple in their wedding vows. The music, the throwing of rice—all felt very familiar and comfortable. Later during the service Pastor Adamo baptized the couple's young child. The pastor's appearance had a Puritan-like plainness, a simple ministerial robe. He preached on John 15: "These things I have spoken to you, that my joy may be in you, and that your joy may be full." This seemed appropriate for a beautiful Sunday morning with a wedding and a baptism.

At the conference I spoke after Domenico Maselli, an esteemed elder spokesman for Protestants in Italy, a pastor, politician, professor, and scholar. Maselli spoke, or so it seemed when I glanced at the paper he held, from one page of handwritten notes and yet he delivered an animated lecture on the relation between the Catholic Church and other churches in Italy. I followed Maselli with my specific case study of one particular Southern evangelization. Massimo Rubboli, University of Genoa, arranged the proceedings so that presentations moved from the general to the particular and then back out to analyses of breadth such as the final paper, Anna Maffei's discussion of the Baptist church in Italy today.

I traced the years of my great-grandfather's pastorate in Calitri and his first years in the United States, especially at the Italian Baptist Church of Monson, Massachusetts. I then turned my talk back to Italy, but the Italy of 2013 and not that of 1913, and asked if Protestantism in a predominantly Catholic country might hinder Italianization, whereas Protestantism in the America of a century ago might have been an aid to Americanization? I noted that the mission churches of a century ago in the United States all offered many social programs for immigrants. Now that Italy has become a country of in-migration rather than out-migration how has this change impacted the small, but vibrant, Protestant communities of Italy? All the Italian American Protestant churches at the beginning of the prior century offered abundant social and educational services. Is this so for Protestant churches and the current situation in Italy? What, I asked, can the Protestant churches in Italy do for today's immigrants?

Before the lunch break finished, I walked through the Theology School with Marta D'Auria, a journalist. We looked for a quiet place to talk. In the library she asked me questions, one of which concerned the lasting impact of my great-grandfather or the relevance that he might have for today. I thought of the Waldensian's motto once more, the Waldensians who are the oldest reform Christian faith, having begun in the last half of the twelfth century—long before Martin Luther—and faced centuries of persecution stretching long after the time of the Protestant Reformation. I thought of the nine days Rev. Alfredo Barone spent in jail for preaching the gospel in the small hill town of Trevico.

Had I more time for my lecture, I might have read my adaptation of a poem by contemporary Neapolitan writer Erri De Luca which begins: "In the Straits of Otranto and Sicily, / Migrants without voice, / Workers from Africa and Asia" and ends ". . . for them: / The miracle of Italy is a curse. / For nothing, they're left to drown." Thank God I did not have more time. For besides the past, beside family history—what gives me the right to challenge the Protestants of Italy? What do I know of the hungry of Rome or of Hartford? What do I know of the drowned so close to the shores of Lampedusa? How can I understand the feelings of a young evangelist packing up his family, including a boy who would become my grandfather, and emigrating from Italy to Connecticut in 1899?

In this book I examine the complex history of the lived experience of people who engaged in an alternative religious practice in their homeland and then navigated traditional and dominant ways in their adopted land. My study uses literary sources, church records, manuscript sources, and secondary sources in various fields to recover many forgotten voices such as the Baptist Antonio Mangano and the Methodist Antonio Arrighi. Additionally, throughout this project that weaves together Italy and the United States is the story of Rev. Alfredo Barone, my great-grandfather, especially his leadership of Baptist churches in Calitri, Italy and Monson, Massachusetts. I seek to offend no faith tradition, to respect all, and to celebrate at the same time that I analyze and critique.

I title this book *Beyond Memory* because so many want to rob Italian Americans of any trace of Italian identity and push them into the ranks of the Yankee Doodle Dandies: *Beyond Memory* because "all Italians are Catholic," because it is little known that this is not so, because Italian American Protestant churches are gone: and *Beyond Memory* because it is difficult to recall this somewhat forgotten past. For example, the Italian Branch of the Assemblies of God incorporated in New Jersey in 1951 and grew thereafter until first the use of the Italian language declined, and then in 1990 the specifically Italian Pentecostal organization dissolved (Saggio 40). Today in Italy, according to figures from Marco Giampetruzzi (archivist Unione Cristiana

Evangelica Battista d'Italia, Rome), there are 112 churches in the Union of Baptists and 4,275 members. This does not take into account Baptists of other umbrella organizations such as Reformed Baptists and other free Baptists churches. More than a century ago (1909) Rev. D. G. (Dexter) Whittinghill counted 60 Baptist churches in Italy with 1,619 members ("The Italian Mission" 170), while in his 1918 study Enrico Sartorio reported, "There are in America about four hundred Italian Protestant churches and missions, having a membership of more than twenty-five thousand Italians" (110). Although these numbers are low, the Italian Protestants at the time of migration and after can tell us much about Italy, America, and religion. Even the fact that Catholics often referred to Protestant evangelization as a failure, whereas Protestants almost always called it promising, reveals something important about the attitudes of both groups regarding the evangelization efforts of the latter. The differing attitudes toward these numbers are discussed in this volume's subsequent pages.

My book focuses on religion (though more the mainline rather than Pentacostal faiths), and considers contradictions in the lived experience of Italian-Americans. An obvious contradiction right from the get-go is the erroneously popular belief that all Italians are Catholics. Even if that were true, what would it mean? What does that *are* include and exclude? In this study I examine first (in chapter 1) the complex history of Italian-American Protestants, especially during the peak years of immigration. Through the use of a wide variety of sources, including spiritual autobiographies, archival material, and Italian American fiction, I argue that Protestantism became a means to negotiate old world and new world ways more than it resulted in the double alienation of rejection by Catholic immigrants and condescension by Anglo-Protestants. Italian American Protestants retained a sense of *italianità* (a term used in Italian American studies to denote the recovery of Italian cultural identity) at the same time that they became American. As a pamphlet published in 1936 by the Chicago Italian Presbyterian Church put it: "it has been the Protestant church with its liberal, social, and educational program that has offered the greatest promise of successful conservation of the Italian culture in Chicago. It has been the Protestant institution, with its practical, rather than ritualistic, ministry that is playing the leading part in the Christian Americanization process so vital to the welfare of city and nation" ("City Country Family Church").

The motive behind the actions of immigrants or ethnics may not simply be an ever-marching move into the mainstream coupled with a shedding of the distinct characteristics that make them different than those in the dominant group. Stefano Luconi, for example, has argued that for many Italian Americans during the interwar years, "their naturalization and participation in the US electoral process did not arise from acculturation or from the intention to get assimilated. Rather, it resulted from the retention of strong ethnic ties to their ancestral country that fascism endeavored to manipulate to its own benefit" (7). In other words, some Italian Americans registered to vote in America so that they could support the interests of the Italian nation.

If in the US conversion to Protestantism could have meant a move into the mainstream, the motivation—at least for ministers—seems rarely to have been attempted for material reward and to undertake such a calling always included some risk. Consider briefly the experience of Rev. Alfredo Barone at the start of the twentieth century and that of Rev. Linda Mercadante much later in the century. Rev. Barone named his first American born son William Walker Barone. That may sound like an assimilationist practice, but that would be a superficial reading of the name, for William is the English version Guglielmo, Alfredo's father's first name, and Walker signifies here not an American cowboy in the West, but Alfredo's English Baptist mentor, Rev. Robert Walker. This child died after little more than two months. After this child, Alfredo and Rosina returned to their practice of using Biblical names for their children such as Maherashalhashbay (1903), hardly a name to help a child fit in nicely at their American grammar school.

Alfredo preached in Haverhill, Massachusetts, upon arrival in the US and then for a period in Monson. After Monson he moved on to Lawrence and Stamford, Connecticut. Then something strange and inexplicable happened. He separated from the Baptist Church. According to my grandfather, "In 1910, because of 'lack of funds' he [Alfredo] was set adrift by the Home Mission Society of this country, without means of support" ("Obituary"). But this makes no sense for in 1910 he still continued as minister of the Italian Baptist Church in Stamford and a child, Dorcas, was born that year in Monson. Could it be that my grandfather has the wrong date here for the split, and could the separation have been initiated by Rev. Alfredo and not the Baptist Church? Alfredo attended regional meetings of Baptist ministers such as a large gathering in 1901 at Springfield and a smaller one a few years later in Newark, but after a time his name falls off the list of attendees at such gatherings. Baptist evangelization of Italians had been vigorous during the years just before the Great War and the Baptists felt a great need for evangelists to the Italian immigrants. Why would they set Rev. Alfredo "adrift"? Could it be that Rev. Barone found a leader such as Rev. Antonio Mangano too American and not enough Italian? Alfredo Barone never became a citizen of the United States.

Linda Mercadante, on the other hand, was born in New Jersey to an Italian Catholic father and a mother of East European Jewish background. As a child, much to her mother's chagrin, Linda Mercadante became a Catholic. Linda, though, had a complex faith journey that eventually led her to become an ordained Presbyterian minister. Along this journey she never took a single step for privilege or prestige. After college she became a United Airlines stewardess—a choice she made to fit in with her current world and the expectations for a woman in that world. When she became a Protestant, however, a cousin's husband asked her, "'What now, you're not going to eat *scungilli* anymore?'" and Linda notes that she did feel "disloyal" (140). She states, "While my conversion made *me* feel whole, it seemed to be separating me even further from others" (140). Once again, one doesn't necessarily undertake such moves to move into the mainstream.

When she becomes not just a Protestant but also a Presbyterian minister, her complex feeling of separation and wholeness remains. She notes that her parents came to her ordination in 1987 and "[. . .] it felt weird that they were watching me do something so aberrant to their backgrounds" (173). At the end of her spiritual memoir she concludes, "I guess I'll never be the archetypal WASP" (203), and she affirms, "I have not deserted my roots but have incorporated them into a new thing" (208). The ideology of Americanization has been one thing and the lived experience of Italian Protestant pastors, another. Sometimes they converged; sometimes, diverged. Nonetheless, the ideal of Americanization rarely corresponded to the realities of daily life.

In chapter 2 I turn to Italy and describe the many difficulties of being a Protestant there, the double binds and catch-22's that confronted such a person. For example, I assert (and explain) that "if Catholics rejected Italian Protestant ministers for being irreligious, liberals of the new nation's political structure rejected them for being too religious." Next, in chapter 3, I try to place the discussion of Italian Protestantism in the context of the Southern Question (the abuse and exploitation of the region south of Rome by the powers north of Rome). If placed in this context, why did Protestantism appeal to some Southern Italians? This chapter argues that whereas Italian Protestantism was an alternative expression of faith and spirituality to the authoritarianism of Catholicism, in America Protestantism became for some a conservative vehicle of nationalism and assimilation. Through an analysis of Protestantism and the South, an anti-Protestant backlash in the South, the interplay of religious and political exile, and science and Protestantism, this chapter considers the manufacture of national identity and how cultural appropriation can be a pathway to assimilation, prosperity, and citizenship.

Chapter 4 considers responses from Catholics and Protestants to the conflict in the late nineteenth century between the Catholic Church and the liberal Italian state. This chapter, as well as the previous, considers the intersection of economics, politics, and religion. Protestants in America thought the defeat of papal troops and the incorporation of the papal states into a unified Italy a great expression of freedom and democracy. Catholics in Italy were divided in their support of either the Pope or the national government. However, the Catholic establishment in America vigorously opposed the Italian state and believed that the Pope had been imprisoned by it. This put Italian immigrants to the United States in an awkward position. In this chapter I use contemporary sources such as the Methodist minister Antonio Arrighi's autobiography and later work such as American novelist Pietro di Donato's biography of Mother Cabrini. The accords of 1929 between the Italian government and the Vatican may have resolved the Roman Question, yet intense feelings regarding this history still surface in writings by Protestants, Catholics, Americans, and Italians.

In the chapter 5, I discuss one particular Italian Protestant minister, Alfredo Barone, and his missions in both Italy (especially Calitri, Avellino) and the United States (especially Monson, Massachusetts). Occasionally, my discussion moves back and forth from Italy to the United States (as many preachers and their congregants did), and it moves from preachers in general to one example, Barone, and later (chapter 6) from churches in general to one in particular, the Italian Congregational Church of Hartford, Connecticut, and then finally in the last chapter to church structure and what took place in those churches especially as exemplified in sermons. Chapter 5 follows Rev. Barone from his ministry in and around Calitri, Italy during the 1890s to his work in Massachusetts and Connecticut in the early twentieth century. Herein I investigate the cultural transition associated with ministries to immigrant communities and how they impact the life cycle of the ethnic church, especially for those immigrant populations that are not replenished over time.

I then turn from one minister and two churches to take a close look at one particular church, the Italian Congregational Church of Hartford. Remember: the Congregational Church was once the state church for Connecticut. Many leading Connecticut native citizens such as Joseph Twichell (Mark Twain's pastor) and Joel Ives were involved with the Italian Congregational Church, and so this chapter turns the viewpoint around somewhat like the second chapter does for Southern Italy. Did the Anglo-Congregational authorities control the Italian Church? Did the Italian Church have some influence on the old traditional Connecticut Congregationalism? Chapter 6 shows that the attitude of the Hartford Congregational elite was very similar to that of the English and American missionaries in Italy. The chapter also shows how the immigrant church passes through stages of establishment and the struggle to sustain, and then institutionalization and finally to a gradual fading away due to social and geographic mobility and the curtailment of an ongoing influx of immigrants. The *Hartford Courant* covered this immigrant church from its founding in 1903 until its final pastor, Rev. Natale Ricciardi, retired in 1976. My concern, however, is predominantly with the church's developmental years, which are also the years of high immigration.

Chapter 7 provides a textual analysis of some Italian American Protestant sermons as well as discusses aspects of Italian American homiletics as described in seminary curricula and other archival material. I concentrate on a sermon preached at the American Union Church in Florence, Italy in 1872, and then move to sermons by Luigi Turco at the mid-twentieth century and then to sermons by Arthur Caliandro. Here I talk about change over time and answer the question that if the Italian American churches have all but disappeared, has Italian American Protestantism also disappeared? At the end of his life Luigi Turco (father of well-known poet Lewis Turco) struggled with New Thought theology—an optimistic belief in the power of the mind—and Arthur Calinandro through his mentorship by Rev. Norman Vincent Peale, grew up spiritually, on one-half New Thought theology and one-half Methodist evangelism. Caliandro's "broad appeal"—so the

Marble Collegiate Church website states—"was based on an anecdotal, extemporaneous sermon delivery drawing on personal experiences and observations. This 'take-home value' style of preaching endeared him to the congregation [. . .]" ("Legacy" 1). This minister, who followed in the pastorate of the well-known self-help sermonizer, Norman Vincent Peale, was the son of an Italian immigrant Methodist preacher. Late in life Arthur Caliandro said in his sermon "Jesus is not the Problem": "my father wanted me to hear every evangelist that came through town [. . .] I did not have a good experience and I pushed back" (2). Out of the evangelism of his father and the popularizing of his mentor, did this Italian-American find his way and form his particular genius, one that allowed him to retain a sense of *italianità*?

"Migrants," Graziella Parati has written, "experience a double absence: absent as they are from their country of origin and a familiar culture and pushed into a position of erasure and expendability at the margins of the country of immigration" (25). Italy is a destination culture, a promised land for the early twenty-first century, as America was for the early twentieth century. In the epilogue as well as thinking about contemporary Italy and Protestantism, once again Rev. Alfredo Barone is present. If he represents the heroic for the Barone generations that followed in America, then why did he ignore the cries of his mother back in Italy for help? As I have found in recently discovered postcards, she was left behind in Italy but desired to come to America. She wrote of hardship, but she wrote in nondialect Italian. What to make of all this? The "Epilogue" contains some surprise, as well as summary and some comments on Protestants in Italy today.

∽

In a play written for the Italian Department of the Colgate-Rochester Divinity School, a program founded in 1907 and designed for the training of Italian immigrants as Baptist pastors to minister to the needs of fellow immigrants, one character, Genius, tells another character, Indifferent Spirit, "you ignore the transforming power of the Gospel in a human heart" ("A School of Prophets" 5). How difficult it must be for us today to imagine "the transforming power of the Gospel," especially for that person of Southern Italy, who may hold a book in hand for the first time or, at the very least, is free to read for the very first time—and in the land of such high rates of illiteracy or in the United States where illiteracy becomes compounded by the fact that English rather than Italian is the language of the land, the book one holds in hand to learn to read or to learn to read and to learn English, too, is the Gospel. Did one experience a Protestant Church in order to seek a deeper experience with Christ than available in a priest-mediated Catholic one, or was the enticement of literacy the primary attraction? Alexandra de Luise in her recent work on the Anson Phelps Stokes Italian Free Library in lower Manhattan has written: "Established in July 1894, the catalyst for its fruition was Antonio Arrighi, a Protestant minister and well-known figure in the community. While the supposed mission of the library was to educate and socialize the Italian immigrant into the New World, so to speak, Arrighi also capitalized on it by identifying those ready for religious conversion and hence, Americanization" (1).

Or try to imagine railroad construction midway between Naples and Bari in the ancient hill town of Calitri, where a young, slight, bearded Protestant preacher gathers a handful of tired workers and preaches to them. As Rev. Robert Walker of the Baptist Missionary Society of England reported in 1893, "A colporteur-evangelist, Signor Barone, has been able to initiate a most hopeful movement. In October, nine men were publicly baptized in the River Ofanto, confessing their faith in the Savior" (*Annual Report of the Committee* 91). D. W. Bebbington stated at the 150 Years of Baptist Witness conference that for the English and American Baptists, "their firm Evangelicalism made them want to carry the gospel to new lands and their stern anti-Catholicism made Italy a likely target" ("Early Developments" 27). Motives for belief and practice, in other words, are often complex and rarely simple and straightforward. Why did some Italians and Italian Americans turn to Protestantism? In answering this question, I consider Protestantism in relation to Catholicism (both in the United States and Italy) and to Americanization. Although the numbers of Italian Protestants whether in contemporary Italy or in New York during the high tide of immigration (1890–1920) have always been small, the impact and what the movement can tell us is large. My study considers in addition to Americanization efforts of the early-twentieth-century global migrations of populations across the past 150 years, the relationship between religion and nation, and the interstices of materialism and spirituality.

One of the reasons to write such a book must be to deepen our understanding of the past and broaden our view of the present: in other words, to counter stereotypes and enrich experience. Too often words will make rigid that which the world keeps ever in flux and when we try to solidify something fluid in speech all too often we end in contraction. Some say all Italians are Catholic, and some say all Italians are involved in some way with the Mafia. While the latter is said with malice, for every speaker knows it is not true, the former may be said in complete innocence or ignorance. Food, faith, and family are the concerns of Italian Americans, we so often hear, and yet look at the classic of Italian American experience Pascal D'Angelo's *Son of Italy*. In this memoir of early-twentieth-century immigrant life there are very few references to family and food, and one has to stretch one's interpretation to see any faith other than a sort of abstract and secular faith in America. "I had learned the great lesson of America," D'Angelo says, "I had learned to have faith in the future" (156). One poem he titles "Omnis Sum," which might have a religious ring to it since they are Latin words, except that those two words mean "I am all" (and not, for example, "God is all").

The persistent presence of a Protestant strain and influence has been an overlooked aspect of Italian migration to America and its relation to religion. For example, in the entire run of the *Journal of Presbyterian History*, there has been only one published article on the topic: John B. Macnab's 1977 essay on Presbyterians and Italian Americans in New York City. Linda Mercandante and Charles Scalise have published short essays on Italian American Protestants, Constantine Panuzio and Angelo di Domenica in particular, in recent issues of *Italian Americana*. There are a few pages of general summary lacking significant interpretation on Luigi Turco, Antonio Arrighi, and Constantine Panunzio in Ilaria Serra's 2007 book, *The Value of Worthless Lives: Writing Italian American Immigrant Autobiographies* (104–111).

I regard myself primarily as a literary historian, not a historian of religion or a sociologist. And so my sources begin with those of a literary nature: novels such as *The Fortunate Pilgrim* and *The Right Thing to Do*, memoirs such *The Story of Antonio, the Galley Slave* and *Protestant Witness of a New American*, sermons by Luigi Turco and Arthur Caliandro, and letters by many. Other sources, such as mission reports and newspaper articles, are of a more historical nature. Many of the books mentioned herein are most likely available on Google Books, but I still like the material artifact, and it is the Internet that has so readily allowed me to obtain so many of these gems. For example, I purchased Christian McLeod's (pen name for Anna Ruddy) *The Heart of a Stranger: A Story of Little Italy* from AbeBooks, and when it came there was a note inside with it. I had purchased the book unknowingly from Gil Williams's bookstore in Binghamton, New York. I knew Gil many years ago when he ran his small literary press and produced some beautiful books and broadsides. Many of my sources come from archives across the globe, from Atlanta to Rome. My study uses extensive primary sources on religion, immigration, and Americanization. E-mail has enabled me—a person not particularly fond of travel—to access so much from such a wide range of places. I have interviewed Italian American preachers and corresponded with the children and grandchildren of other preachers.

From this multitude of sources I quote extensively. I love their voices and their ability to evoke, I believe, a past. Remember: these are more or less forgotten voices, and even if remembered (Mario Puzo, let's say), the passage I quote (or summarize) most certainly is not one that their fame hangs on. My favorite source is an obscure primary one: could anything be more obscure—or more fascinating—than Antonio Mangano's 1899 Brown University student commencement address! My work avoids contemporary theoretical terminology, yet I am not naive enough to think my writing free of theory; but rather than place the preachers of the past in a postmodern interpretative frame of analysis, here I try to reveal something of their voices.

I seek neither to exonerate the past nor to praise unduly the present. Questions come to mind when considering a dominant narrative in American ethnic studies of the past two decades. Has the lens begun to cloud our vision of the past, forcing the primacy of primary sources to become secondary as the particulars of any past must be shaped into this master narrative or lest the work risks being considered illegitimate? And if made to fit, then the immigrant once again has his or her voice silenced; this time, by the powerful of the present who insist that anything said in that past fit some present scheme of things. Is the current mode of explanation a paradigm or an enclosure? In these pages, voices are recovered more than funneled into preexisting theory. Are not the facts of the migrations and attempted conquests spectacular enough in themselves?

Alfredo Barone preached the gospel despite physical blows and brief imprisonment for having done so, and yet he seems to have abandoned his mother in dire straits in Italy. Rev. Caliandro compromised and changed his given name from Arturo to Arthur, but he ministered to New York's gay and lesbian population and brought women into leadership positions in his church at a time when such actions were a direct challenge to the Protestant elite status-quo.

I recall that when in the year 2000 Jim Murphy published *Pick & Shovel Poet: The Journeys of Pascal D'Angelo*, a sort of adolescent picture book version of D'Angelo's autobiography, I was very perplexed. I found it strange that this book, which usurped—in my view—D'Angelo's words and story appeared in print when the actual book itself had not been republished (except in an Arno Press reprint) since its initial 1924 publication date. When Guernica Editions did republish *Son of Italy* in 2003, Carl Van Doren's introduction to the original edition was omitted. Antonio D'Alfonso, publisher of Guernica Editions, told me, "The introduction was valid back then. Not now. I always find it condescending" (e-mail correspondence with Barone, September 24, 2003). Evaluation slides into judgment too easily. I believe Van Doren's words should have been included. Our knowledge of the past has so many limits. Why go out of the way to increase those boundaries that may bind and blind? Observation is interpretation without the valorization of intellectual domination.

I want to tell their story here, the immigrants', some of them; as well as the story of some of those who would offer the immigrants assistance even if with condescension and complex motives. Also, I write about Baptists, Congregationalists, Episcopalians, and Methodists, so that one denomination must not bear the burden of the entire argument. To try to see the Italian American Protestant from within the world of the early twentieth century differs from looking back one hundred years hence. I seek to return primacy to the vastness of the primary. I have made selections, and these acts of choosing are themselves acts of interpretation.

At the conference in Rome one speaker asked if my work would be an encyclopedia of Italian American Protestantism. And I said no, that would indeed be a valuable project, but, I said, mine would be more a series of case studies. I realized my inaccuracy after speaking to Professor Bebbington. For the book has a story arc to it. The chapters may not be strictly linear but they are tightly interwoven (*text* from the Latin *texere*, to weave). I am a fiction writer and a poet as well as a scholar, and while I strive for scholarly integrity there is also a narrative thrust in this book as it moves from the late nineteenth century to the early twenty-first century.

This book is not a study of the Rev. Alfredo Barone, but his shadow covers all of it, even though according to his 1940s alien identification card he stood a mere five feet and two inches. I should say something here about my vantage point. Peter Biller has written: "Where a medieval historian working and looking forwards in time may well be impressed with the strength of the Waldensians, as they spread further and last longer than other comparable heretical movements, a historian of the Protestant Reformation looking backwards over the Middle Ages may well be conditioned to notice the opposite, that is to say, weakness by comparison with what he or she is most familiar with" (10). Simply put, the intellectual place from which an author begins has a very real impact on where the author ends up. I am a descendant of a key figure in this book. I am a poet-scholar living in Connecticut, and my family religious context is Presbyterianism. Have I, as Biller put it, sat "in front of a word processor" and decided "whether to create a figure mistily shrouded in uncertainty and myth or a figure of archival realism" (14), and if so, what did I decide? Read on.

Then, too, there is the limitation of sources. Once at a colloquium at Yale I asked Pentecostal scholar Grant Wacker why all his sources were urban if, since as he said, Pentecostalism is primarily a rural movement. He replied that urban Pentecostals published materials and so those printed sources that survive are urban even though the movement was rural. In my case there survive boxes and boxes of Italian American church records but relatively few sermons. Indeed, my greatest hope for this present work is that it might lead to subsequent studies. I do not cover the full extent of Italian and Italian American Protestantism. This is a rich field that can nourish many more scholarly endeavors.

I have translated phrases and sentences from Italian primary and secondary sources into English. In some instances I include the Italian original for clarity or emphasis. I thank the editors of the following publications in which some of this work has appeared in earlier forms: chapter 1 as "The Soul of a Stranger: Italy, America, and Italian American Protestants" in *Forum Italicum* 44.1 (2010): 136–155; chapter 2 as "To Struggle for a Place at the Table: Italian-American Protestants in Italy" in *Italian Americana* 30.1 (2012): 70–81; part of chapter 5 as "Alfredo Barone, un colportore ed evangelista battista tra Irpinia e Stati Uniti" in *150 anni di presenza battista in Italia (1863-2013)* (Milan: Biblion edizioni, 2015): 123-137; and another portion of this chapter as "By Twos and by Threes: The Italian Baptist Church at Monson, Massachusetts" in the *American Baptist Quarterly* 28.4 (2009): 413–420. I presented much of this material in conference papers and talks at the John D. Calandra Italian American Institute, Queens College, City University of New York; the Italian American Studies Association Conference; the First Congregational Church of Monson, Massachusetts; Saint James Episcopal Church, West Hartford, Connecticut; and the Waldensian Faculty of Theology, Rome, Italy. The University of Saint Joseph National Endowment for the Humanities fund provided support for this project. And last I thank Bruce Barone, Alexandra de Luise, Deborah Ducoff-Barone, Maria Esposito Frank, Fred Gardaphe, Justin Gottuso, Marco Giampetruzzi, Kathleen Kelly, Stefano Luconi, Elizabeth Messina, Charles Scalise, Mario Toglia, Lewis Turco, Benjamin J. Woodard, and, especially, Denise and Pasquale DiFulco. The Methodist missionary leader William Burt noted in 1909: "Italy needs us so much. The Italians on both sides of the ocean need us" (79). This *need*—real, imagined, and in practice—is what this book is all about.

Chapter 1

The Soul of a Stranger

Complexity and Conversion

Some Italian American evangelists such as Angelo di Domenica converted in Italy, while others such as Luigi Turco converted in America. Italian-American Protestant evangelists defended conversion as a spiritual growth, while others attacked conversion as a gross Americanization, an insincere conversion meant to foster material advancement. Authors of the 1920s, such as Constantine Panunzio and Gino Speranza, considered the benefits of Protestantism in an America often conceived as a Protestant land. Did the small number of Italian Protestant immigrants have an easier time fitting into American society at a time period when many proclaimed America a distinctly Protestant country? In Italian American literature, Protestant missionaries or converts appear in various depictions from Anna Ruddy's (Christian McLeod's) *The Heart of a Stranger* (1908) through Mario Puzo's *The Fortunate Pilgrim* (1964) to Helen Barolini's *Umbertina* (1979). Ruddy's positive depiction may result from her missionary Protestantism, and Puzo's negative depiction may result from his Catholicism. Sometimes these converts return to Italy, to reminiscence about the homeland, such as Giuseppe Canzoneri, or like Angelo di Domenica they return to commence a cautious crusade for Protestantism. These stories that appear off to the side if not offstage in Italian American history (think of Jerre Mangione's Protestant uncle, for example, a minor presence in two memoirs) are complex. What is the relation of such evangelists or converts to America and to Italy? Are they Americanized through

Protestantism or doubly alienated: strangers from America because they are immigrants from Italy, and strangers from other Italian immigrants because they are no longer Catholic?

Near the end of Helen Barolini's classic Italian American family saga, *Umbertina*, the great-granddaughter of the magisterial and determined title character feels "as if her old ancestor, the Umbertina she had fruitlessly sought in Castagna, had suddenly become manifest in the New World and spoken to her" (408). Those tiny two words *as if* are crucial ones. At the Ellis Island Museum of Immigration, Umbertina may reach across time to her namesake Tina, but the latter does not fully recognize or identify that metaphoric grasp. All remains tangential, "as if. . . ." Tina looks at the beautiful bedspread that belonged to her great-grandmother and that an Italian Protestant mission worker, Anna Giordani, had obtained through some questionable trickery. Tina believes, "'Calabria—that's where my grandmother's people were from. In fact I'm named for the immigrant named Umbertina. She should have brought such a spread with her—isn't it gorgeous! Then it would have passed down to me, maybe'" (407). "Should have," "maybe," and "as if"—history speaks, but tentatively and tangentially. Readers of *Umbertina* understand the message more fully than the character in the story. We see the ironies and are moved by them, our recognition of them. Tina sees her great-grandmother's bedspread, but Tina doesn't know it. Tina does not know that the bedspread she sees actually did belong to her great-grandmother. If shadow covers all (*terra di ombra*), how will we ever know our past?

I want to know my great-grandparent Alfredo Barone's story. As I read about Italian American Protestants of the early twentieth century or the few specific documents of Alfredo's that I have in my room—the equivalent of Umbertina's *coperta* at the museum—do I hear only tentatively, tangentially: a strange echo, unclear and imprecise in its reverberations? "I read these articles as history. But also as a cave drawing on the inner walls of my own skull," Paul Auster said about reading of his grandparents' turbulent lives (37).

Temporal distance necessitates the time machine for truth seekers. In the early twentieth century, Monson, Massachusetts nearly had as many immigrant residents as its entire population today. "On October 18, 1904, delegates of the Westfield Baptist Association voted to receive the Monson Italian Baptist Church into fellowship. This little chapel at the Quarry was made possible by the untiring efforts of the Reverend

Alfred Barrone [*sic*]" (*History of Monson* 18). When I went there a few years ago and walked its streets, including one named Thompson, where my great-grandmother lived with her children while her evangelist husband proselytized in a different state, I did not see the chapel or the house or any sign of the immigrant crowd of yesteryear; nor could I imagine it, any of it, whatever it was. But from a multiplicity of texts, a message and a pattern may emerge: Italian American Protestantism as a negotiation between adopting the demands of Americanization and maintaining a cherished *italianità*. Robert Orsi believes that novelist Garibaldi M. Lapolla's "critique of American values is cast as a scathing satire of Protestant missionary activity [. . .]" (159) in the 1933 novel *The Grand Gennaro*. Yet, Lapolla does not depict the Protestants in a completely negative light. Although "to invite the Italians to sit with them in the gorgeous pews of their splendid edifices—that was another matter indeed" (172), Lapolla also states, on the other hand, that "the work done [by the Protestant missions] was often the means of saving many a family from sheer wretchedness and squalor, if not from starvation" (173). Lapolla modeled his fictional character, Emma Reddle, on the actual missionary Anna Ruddy. Lapolla's very mixed depiction differs from educator Leonard Covello's, who named an award at the high school he led in honor of Ruddy. Miss Ruddy, Covello says, "was a tremendous influence in East Harlem during a lifetime devoted to the cause of the recently arrived immigrant and his children" (32) and, he concluded, "in the unfolding of our lives, Miss Ruddy and the Home Garden filled a need we could find nowhere else" (34).

At any rate, the history of Italian American Protestantism is very complex in its accounting. In their introduction to the essay collection *The Lost World of Italian-American Radicalism*, Philip V. Cannistraro and Gerald Meyer state that, "conversion to Protestantism was not an option for most Italians" (11). I would add that radicalism, which they say "provided an alternative to religion" (11), was also not an option for most Italians. Protestantism, like radicalism, may have originated, at least in part, in reaction to the authority of the Catholic Church and out of the liberalizing trends that led to and continued after the reunification of Italy. Both Italian American radicalism and Italian American Protestantism are somewhat less-discussed topics in Italian American studies. The former was seen by many as an affront to hard-earned mainstream American respectability. The latter may be ignored because of commonplace notions regarding the collapsing of the Italian and

Catholic identity. As friends invariably said to me when I told them about this project: aren't all Italian Americans Catholic? Similarly, near the start of their introduction, Cannistraro and Meyer say, "For most Americans, Italian American radicalism is an oxymoron" (2).

Just as during the years of peak immigration there were many and important Italian radicals, so, too, were there Italian Protestants. And just as radicalism relied on trans-Atlantic and transnational connection (Cannistraro and Meyer 5), so, too, did Protestantism. Rev. Agide Pirazzini, for example, noted an interesting mixed condition of Italian pastors: "Italian students for the ministry are generally divided into two great classes: Those who have lived and studied chiefly in Italy, and who therefore need to be Americanized; and those who have lived and studied chiefly in America and therefore need to be Italianized" (152–153). Cannistraro and Meyer believe that their work indicates that "the illiteracy of Italian immigrants in general has been exaggerated" (13). I agree with this observation, for every little storefront church, every evangelical tent meeting had its publication, usually in Italian, sometimes in Italian and some English and, if long-lasting, often reversing over time its proportion of Italian and English. I would add that the number of Protestants, like those of radicals—though again for contrasting reasons—might be underestimated. In his study of Italian emigration and its use in nation building, Mark I. Choate notes how the Italian Catholic church labored to maintain and strengthen ties with emigrants. He says that among the questions that authorities in Italy deliberated—questions that make a direct connection between Protestantism and radicalism—are these: "Should the church help immigrants learn English, and improve their prospects for success in their new homeland? Or might immigrants avoid church services in a language they did not understand and turn to Italian Protestants or Italian Socialists and anarchists for solidarity?" (136). The Protestants, like the radicals, must have had some success. Anna Ruddy, at the end of her fictionalized account of the Home Garden mission in East Harlem, offers the Protestant mission as a means to escape from the clutches of mobsters and anarchists, a different and better source of identity and community (211–215). In a newsletter of April 1916, Rev. Alfredo Barone claimed to have 2,000 members in his Alpha and Omega Assembly stretching across four states: New Jersey, New York, Connecticut, and Massachusetts.

Why do I call these Protestants radical? After all, forsaking Catholicism for a Protestant faith during the heyday of immigration to the United States can be seen as a safe choice, an easy move toward quick assimilation. Some Italian Protestant leaders thought it not so much safe, as absolutely necessary. Sounding the bell of Anglo conformity, Rev. Angelo di Domenica in a 1918 essay claimed "[. . .] the Protestant forces in America ought to come together and study all the ways and means to do a real aggressive work [. . .]. The work must be done, not only for the salvation of the Italians, but for the salvation of America as well" ("Sons of Italy" 191). Connecticut-born (to Italian immigrant parents) Gino Speranza, a lawyer involved in settlement house work in New York City, similarly thought America a Protestant nation and, therefore, "the closer the likeness of mind and character of its people, the better will the American democracy function [. . .] the greater the divergences and differences from the historic homogeneity of the American people, the greater the strain upon American civilization" (27).

During the latter nineteenth century in Italy, anti–Catholic Church sentiment steadily increased and in the years after Unification, Baptist, Methodist, and Presbyterian missionaries proselytized from end to end of the peninsula. The long-surviving Waldensians provided a rich Protestant heritage in the land of the Papal See. But, as Choate has shown, a countertrend also emerged. "Before World War I," according to Choate, "Italian Catholic missionaries with critical Vatican support eased the transition of emigrants into the disorienting religious and social climate of the Americas. Though bitter enemies at home, the Catholic Church and Italian state were able to work together to 'make Italians,' and Catholics, in emigrant colonies abroad" (145).

To convert to a Protestant faith in either the liberalizing reunified Italy or in the self-proclaimed land of the religiously free (a land actually supremely rich in prejudice) required great self-sacrifice. This is why I call the Protestant converts "radical." Italian born, and educated at Colgate and Brown universities, Baptist Antonio Mangano said quite simply, "It takes much courage and strong conviction to join a Protestant church, for alienation from friends and relatives may follow [. . .]" (*Sons of Italy* 207). Rev. Antonio Arrighi notes that after his conversion, he "was formally disowned at law for disobedience to the will of my parents, and also by the [Catholic] Church as a heretic" (221).

While the Catholic priest Aurelio Palmieri warned in 1918 that "long experience proves that Italians either are or have to be Catholics, else they will ramble about the labyrinth of an ungodly materialism" (177), becoming a Protestant preacher did not lead to earthly wealth, nor did these men lose their way in pursuit of material extravagances. As Luigi Turco recorded in his autobiography, "my financial condition has always been poor" ("Brief Story" 9). Turco, like other converts, noted that when he grew up in Italy "the prestige of the Roman Catholic Church was very low. The only thing I heard about it was the corruption of priests and nuns" ("Postscript" 232). When he did become Baptist: "A terrific persecution was started against me by my sister and her husband [. . .] I wrote to my father in Italy [. . .] He thought that I was getting insane" ("Brief Story" 4).

Invariably, in America the converted would be scorned by family and friends and kept at a distance by Anglo Protestants. The Methodist Constantine Panunzio, near the end of his autobiography *The Soul of an Immigrant* (1921), recalls, "one case where a young man was cast out of his home by his parents because they did not approve of his attending the meetings held in our little chapel. He came very near going insane under the strain" (204). Panunzio notes on the very same page that his supervisors in Boston were not really concerned with the welfare of Italians, they just wanted a good show of numbers, and the people in charge, Panunzio says, lacked any understanding of immigrant culture. In a brief biographical sketch of Alfredo Barone, my grandfather Melchisedec Barone noted that after conversion: Alfredo "was disowned by his aristocratic parents. From that day on he spread the Gospel throughout Italy when it was hazardous to do so. He was stoned, imprisoned, and an attempt [was] made to burn him to the stake." Panunzio makes no mention in his autobiography of the particular Protestant faith he served and practiced: this imprecision may be a peculiarly Italian Protestant trait. My great-grandfather never became a United States citizen even though he lived in the US from 1899 until his death in 1950. These religious radicals wanted to retain some connection to their Italian past, even as they moved, successfully, into their American future.

Panunzio may not have mentioned his specific Protestant faith because these ministers and their congregants maintained an energetic fluidity rather than a strict sectarianism. In the "Foreword" to his autobiography, Panunzio also notes that his "tale depicts *the inner, the soul struggles* of the immigrant more than his outward success or failure" (xi). The Italian immigrant navigated and negotiated the many channels of Christian churches. Alfredo Barone, like other Italian Protestant clergymen, started in a Catholic seminary. He rejected Catholicism and converted to Baptism, went to England for some religious training (according to my grandfather), and returned to Italy. After preaching there for some time, he left for America under the auspices of the Home Mission Society of London (according to my grandfather). After a little more than a decade of service throughout the northeast, he broke with the formal Baptist church and formed his own missionary society. According to my grandfather, he did so due to a severe curtailment in funds from the Baptist missionary society. I believe his cherished Italian identity and his interest in Apocalyptic Prophecy and classical philosophy contributed to his decision to strike out on his own ("Requirements"). (Eleven of his thirteen children had Biblical names: the thirteenth child—known as Bill—received Socrates for his first name.) Michael T. Ward, in an essay about the Waldensians in Texas, mentions the Rev. Arturo D'Albergo, who not only moved from place to place in Italy, and back and forth a few times between the United States and Italy, but served evangelical, Presbyterian, Dutch Reformed, and Waldensian congregations (196).

Some of these Italians converted to Protestantism in Italy (Alfredo Barone) and others in the United States (Constantine Panunzio). Some went back to Italy. Panunzio writes about this return as do others, such as Antonio Arrighi and Antonio Mangano. In his autobiography, Angelo di Domenica, the Angel of Sunday, recalls that when he returned to his hometown, everyone greeted him warmly and he "preached every evening in that church, which had been built where I was born in the flesh and in the faith. It was filled with people at every service" (*Protestant Witness* 160).

One of the returning minister's main concerns was the spiritual health of his family members. The converted preacher (usually disowned by his Catholic family), put conversion of his family at the top of his goals. Luigi Turco, for example, notes that after his conversion (in America) his "first desire [. . .] was to lead" his "unreligious family in America and in Italy to the feet of the Master, The Great Master of Life, Jesus the Christ" ("Brief Story" 4). Twelve years later he returned to Riesi where he preached. During a "great revival," he did convert his family and friends. Similarly, the older brothers of Angelo di Domenica returned from New York to their hometown, Schiavi d'Abruzzo, "to evangelize their family and endeavor to establish a Protestant mission in their native town" (*Protestant Witness* 22). Angelo records: "On the very evening that they arrived home, Vincent and Tony began to preach the Gospel, not only to the members of their family but to the people who came to inquire about relatives who were living in New York. Every evening they held a service, and the people who came to hear them increased daily in numbers and in interest" (*Protestant Witness* 23). After many years of ministerial work in America, especially in Philadelphia, Angelo returned to Italy. Angelo recalls the start of this mission tour that began in Naples: "It was a magnificent sight to see a congregation of nearly two hundred people assembled in that Upper Hall on a hot summer Sunday morning to hear the message of the Gospel from an American pastor" (*Protestant Witness* 158). As noted previously, di Domenica had a triumphal return to his hometown, but he also preached in Boscoreale, Bari, Mottola, Florence, Ariccia, and Rome. He preached up and down the peninsula in big cities and small towns. He preached usually for two hours and sometimes to audiences as large as four hundred. He preached a mix of American civil religion, Italian pride, and evangelical Christianity. So successful was his preaching tour that he planned to return two years later for a full year, but ill health forced him to cancel this much anticipated trip.

The conversion of the ministers themselves followed a standard Protestant progression: recognition of sinfulness, intense self-examination and self-abnegation, rebirth in the spirit, and public testimony. The autobiographies of converts are a part of their testimony and these spiritual self-histories are meant to inspire others. Antonio Arrighi, for example, divides his book of adventures, his tale of captivity and conversion into three sections: the first section describes his time as a drummer boy with Garibaldi's soldiers; the next section narrates the horror of his imprisonment and enslavement in Civita Vecchia, followed by his escape to America; part three tells of his life in America, his conversion and his return to Italy as a Protestant missionary. The first two sections create strong anti-Catholic sentiment. Without any direct criticisms, the Church is viewed as the power behind the injustices that our hero suffers. Recall that in his novel of 1867 Garibaldi said, "the despotism of the tiaraed [*sic*] priests is the most hateful and degrading of all" (11). Nonetheless, the third section follows the conversion form. In Des Moines, Iowa he attends his first Protestant church service. Although he does not understand all that the Methodist preacher says and although he fears he has committed a sin just by entering, he does know that the preacher spoke about "Christ as the true bread of life" (201). He moves to Fairfield, Iowa, and in that town he converts at a revival meeting. Arrighi realizes he too often uses "profanity and harsh speech" (203) and begins to "examine" himself (204). He writes, "As I threw myself on the mercies of God and accepted Jesus as my Great High Priest who had given His life to save me, oh, what sweet peace came to my troubled heart? Joy like a river flowed into my redeemed soul" (207). At the annual meeting of the Iowa Methodist Episcopal Church, Arrighi tells us: "at a certain point I stood up before that body of more than two hundred Christian ministers, and in a simple way gave the history of my conversion" (208).

For di Domenica, sin manifested itself in card playing. "Before my conversion," he writes, "I was addicted to card playing" (*Protestant Witness* 26). His older brother, Vincent, had been a card player, too, but after conversion Angelo's brother never played cards again. Angelo tells his brother that he, too, has forsaken card playing, but this is a lie. "For several weeks," after his lie, Angelo says, "I was tormented every night, because in my dreams I was playing cards [. . .]. I was desperate; I did not know just what to do; I could not rest" (*Protestant Witness* 27). He turns to prayer and after three months: "I gave my heart to Jesus Christ who gave me peace and rest. Ever since that time I have never handled cards" (*Protestant Witness* 27). Similarly, Turco reports that "a few months after my conversion God gave me the power to stop smoking, drinking, and unlegal [sic] sexual relations" ("Brief Story" 4).

Many of the Italian Protestant ministers claim a nominal and corrupt Catholicism as a reason for their conversion. Panunzio, for example, describes his childhood religious education as "very limited, almost a negligible factor [. . .]" (18). He says that religion "was considered primarily a woman's function" (18). He continues: "We children continuously heard our male relatives speak disparagingly of religion, if religion it could be called. They would speak of the corruption of the Church" (18). The Confirmation ritual for Panunzio, only meant a new suit and some sweets, and "the thing itself [. . .] excited no concern" in his thoughts (44). When he arrived for study at a Catholic seminary, he found it "like a dungeon," "a tomb" (48). Mangano noted, "it is erroneous to suppose that because a man has spent ten or twelve years in a seminary for priests, he is an educated man" (*Sons of Italy* 48).

"Ritualism and true spirituality exclude each other," according to di Domenica (*Protestant Witness* 75). He says: "The ritualism of the Roman Church has smothered all true spirituality" (*Protestant Witness* 74). Even though Panunzio could not understand the preacher's words the first time he heard "a zealous young Baptist preacher," "something strange gripped [his] soul" (134). He stays at the home of a "devout and practical Christian" couple that prays before meals and reads Scripture. "Their religion," Panunzio writes, "was a matter of everyday use and this impressed me profoundly" (143). For Panunzio, alive and soulful preaching, the study of Biblical texts, acts of practice rather than ritual: these as well as the perceived half-heartedness of Catholicism inspired conversions. Robert Canzoneri records his preacher father testifying regarding his conversion: "'I don't call any man father but my own father, live in Sicily still. God is the Father, not somebody in a collar turn 'round say hocus pocus you don't even know what it is'" (100). This statement by the senior Canzoneri contains a forceful appeal to individualism and straight talk.

Social Services and Soul Searching

Two matters, Americanization and preaching in Italian or English, were much debated by Protestant and Catholic missionaries. Choate, for example, notes how Bishop Scalabrini worried that "the emigrants' identities as Italians and Catholics needed to be cherished, buttressed, and promoted by Italian and American prelates" (133). A rapid Americanization, some Catholic officials believed, might destroy the emigrants' religious faith and practice (134).

Many of the Protestant clergy debated the use of Italian and the different needs for different generations regarding the language. Panunzio notes that he became Americanized precisely because of separation from all Italian colonies (251). "Immigrant colonies as they now stand," he claims, "are impenetrable citadels, whose invisible walls no amount of Americanization can batter down" (256). For di Domenica, "The real American spirit is the production of Protestantism, anything foreign to it does not mix" (*Protestant Witness* 154). The logic behind this claim is simple: "America was founded upon Christian principles such as were conceived by people of Protestant faith; hence anything which is not in harmony with the Protestant ideal is foreign to America" (*Protestant*

Witness 137). Like Speranza, di Domenica asserts, "In proportion as the Protestant church fails to evangelize the foreigners, in that proportion the foreigners will 'foreignize' America" (*Protestant Witness* 137). In this section of his autobiography, he offers the strangest proof of the success of Protestant Americanization and assimilation. He notes that many people associate Italians with criminals and specifically with gangsters, but, di Domenica writes, "I am glad to tell you that, insofar as I know, there has not been one Italian gangster of Protestant faith who has suffered capital punishment in this country" (*Protestant Witness* 138).

Ruddy draws on criminal sensationalism at the end of her autobiographical novel *The Heart of the Stranger*: if not the mob (she makes use of the Black Hand earlier in the story), then the anarchists. One of the favored youths at the mission house, who has mysteriously disappeared, returns secretively at the novel's end. The boy's treacherous father has forced Luigi into committing violent acts. " 'Miss Lindsay,' " Luigi declares in the novel's moment of highest drama, " 'I am an anarchist!' " (211). He has lost all hope. Miss Lindsay reassures him, " 'There is a way out. Jesus Christ can reach down to where you are now and take you out just as He did before [the time Luigi ran into trouble with the mob]. You are not too far lost for Him to find and save' " (212). According to Ruddy, "The forces of heaven and hell were arrayed against each other for the possession of a human soul, and so strong was the battle that one could almost hear the noise of combat" (214). They kneel in prayer "and when they arose from their knees his face was radiant with joy" (214). Though Luigi's future remains uncertain as he slinks off into the night, he tells Miss Lindsay before leaving the mission house, " 'You are the truest friend a boy ever had' " (215).

Yet, the mission settlement house frequently promoted Americanization more than the advancement of one's spirituality. Ruddy's fictionalized Garden Settlement appeals to city youth by the nontheological means of popular music and sports. Music works because the boys are "little music loving Italians" (96). "The ability to appreciate good music, which others acquired by training and culture," Ruddy states, "came to them naturally as their rightful heritage" (96). Hence, Miss Lindsay seems ever "at the piano" (110). Isabel Fielding, famed for her voice, joins the mission staff: "she wielded untold influence over the children of a music-loving race" (198). But music alone and her performance of it cannot suffice to reign in these little devils of the street. "There was much that she could do for the boys," according to Ruddy, "but a young man of the right stamp, whose example could safely be followed, could do infinitely more." That right man is: "Lloyd, the captain of Columbia's famous eleven who had beaten Yale in the football field the year before" (111). These mission leaders sacrifice much to serve others. Robert Lloyd abandons his old family firm on Wall Street for the less earthy, more heavenly "business of soul-winning" (198).

Various activities beyond the bounds of religious services and instruction became central to the Italian American Protestant churches and their missions. In his work from the 1930s, *Protestant Missions to Catholic Immigrants*, Theodore Abel (an immigrant from Poland and a Columbia University professor) rhetorically asks: "Is the social program consistent with the main purpose of mission work, or does it imply that the churches are promoting a new objective which is non-religious in character?" (11). He finds that the social program, as he puts it, meets church needs and aids the church by attracting members and, at the same time, builds character and better social relationships (11). He considers the school programs for young children and such activities as "sports and home-craft" to be especially important for the second generation (12).

Abel's conclusions resemble the prescriptions of Mangano from a decade and one-half prior and the activities of the Hartford Episcopal Italian Mission, which existed for more than forty years. Mangano said that missions must build "Christlike character in those we aid," but he insisted all activities must be "conducted from a religious point of view" (*Sons of Italy* 149). He warned: "The appeal of the social settlement that ignores religion is to self-interest, a motive not lofty enough to stimulate the development of nobility of character" (*Sons of Italy* 149). His advice seems to mirror precisely what the Hartford mission practiced:

> The ideal method of work is a union of a social settlement ministering to the physical side of life through athletics, health talks, and visiting nurses; to the mental, through clubs and English classes, music, drawing, and handcraft; to the need of fun, through entertainments and social gatherings; and to crown all and give purpose to life, a spiritual ministry, the preaching and teaching of the gospel of Jesus as the way of salvation, by means of religious services,

Sunday-schools, prayer-meetings, and a modern evangelism.
(*Sons of Italy* 149-150)

Such was the form and action of the Hartford Episcopal Italian Mission. Saint Paul's Italian Episcopal Mission aided immigrants in the negotiation of two cultures more than it propelled them to assimilation through Americanization. According to Jon C. Watt, "Those Italians who converted to Pentecostalism, generally, were not seeking to assimilate but rather to maintain their *italianità* in the face of pressure to assimilate" (177). And Choate observes, "By design Italians abroad would learn of their Italian identity, but, more broadly, *italianità* itself would be deepened, defined, and elaborated for Italians at home" (59). The Rev. Paolo Vasquez led such efforts for his congregation to negotiate two cultures. Born in Sicily, he studied for five years in a Catholic seminary. In a July 1915 article, *La Croce*, the Italian/English Episcopal newsletter, informed its readers that Rev. Vasquez left "for personal reasons" (3). At the very beginning of this missionary work, the Sunday school, "that great fundamental adjunct of the church" (*La Croce* 1), had seventy-eight students and a staff of twelve. In the 1920s, the student number would nearly double: a printed report from the mid-1920s notes that there were 130 students in thirteen classes. The report indicates that during the past year there were twenty-nine baptisms, five confirmations, twenty-five marriages, and seven funerals. Church organizations included the following: the girls' friendly club, the communicants' league, the sewing school, the boy scouts, the choir, a music study group, and the St. Paul's Society (a men's club) ("St. Paul's Italian Church").

Within the realm of the sanctuary the report states that certain renovations at Saint Paul's had taken place: "To look through the dark rounded arches of the Rood Screen past the fine oak choir stalls where our little red-vested choir takes its place so well, to the chancel, with its cream walls and white and gold altar, is a bit more inspiring than receiving impressions from white walls and plain windows." In an earlier report of November, 1920, Rev. Vasquez stated, "It is necessary that something be done to give the people of St. Paul's a more churchly Church. It is a vital question, for the growth of the Mission depends largely at the present time upon having a real Church" (Minutes of the Meetings). Rev. Vasquez believed such church improvements crucial because Italians found storefront worship to be nonchurch like given that Catholic churches, especially those in Italy, tend to be ornate and outstanding architectural edifices. Interestingly, the church services "are equally divided in language. Two are held in Italian, that the mature may praise God 'in the beautiful language of the Peninsula,' and in English, that the juniors may praise Him in their adoptive tongue" ("St. Paul's Italian Church"). In the notes of the men's club, English became the standard in late 1947.

In the difficulties St. Paul's and its congregants faced, can be seen aspects of a negotiation between old world and new world ways. In 1920, Rev. Vasquez explained to the Committee in Charge of St. Paul's the importance of an upcoming festival for Italians, the Festa San Paolo. Similarly, in 1925, he wrote the Dean of Christ Church Cathedral to explain why the Italians could not attend a planned service in honor of George Washington: "It is an old custom for the Italians to have dances the week before Lent. In this account most of our Italian people have already pledged their attendance to one social or another" (Letter, February 12, 1925). Rev. Vasquez suggested that the Washington service be held at a later date.

If the church and its congregants sometimes held on to the old ways, on other occasions they adopted the new. In 1920, the summer Sunday school celebrated its completion at the Elizabeth Park playground with every child receiving the treat of an ice cream cone. A month later, on the other hand, the church sponsored a celebration "for the Unification of Italy, at which [there was] a collection made for Italian earthquake relief" (Minutes of the Meetings).

A 1943 fund-raising letter takes a partly defensive tone: "I am impressed by the patriotic spirit that is being manifested there [at St. Paul's] on the part of those people who, either by birth or immediate ancestry, are related to one of the countries with which our country is now at war [. . .]." Then the letter continues: "Thirty-five young men of the Mission are now in the Service with our Armed Forces," and many of the women perform Red Cross work. The letter conflates church and country by asserting that, "these Italian-American young people are being inculcated with that high type of patriotism which has its source and sanction in the Church [. . .]."

When Panunzio returned to Italy in 1918, he proclaimed the land of his birth "wonderful" (302). He closed his eyes because he "could not bear the glory of the sight" (302). When he reached his home, Molfetta, his "relatives and friends asked all kinds of questions about America"

(310). He "spoke of all the good things," but did not tell them about all he "suffered" in America because "they would have been shocked beyond expression" (310). And Panunzio stated, "When they asked my advice about their going to America, I could not honestly council them to do so" (310–311). Yet, when he made a speaking tour of Sicily on behalf of his adopted home, he brought with him "small ribbon American flags, and distributed them by the thousands [. . .]" (322).

Panunzio revealed at the close of his memoir his ongoing conflicted feelings about his adopted land and his homeland. Protestantism offered this immigrant a kind of compass. This memoir, its author wrote, "tells of the agonies and the Calvaries, of the bitter sorrows and high joys of an immigrant soul [. . .]" (xi), and it "shows that even a southern Italian can make something of himself under the inspiring influence of America when he has the proper opportunity and is thrown in the right environment" (xii). Some believed that "proper opportunity" and "right environment" depended on a Protestant foundation; others did not. For some, Protestantism offered a spiritual alternative to a Catholicism perceived to be lackluster and authoritarian; for others it did not.

Italian Protestants in Fiction and Memoir

As spiritual autobiography requires a conversion, so fiction needs its fall guy. In some Italian American fiction and memoir, it is a Protestant character who plays this role. By such narration and character construction, an author of modern secular appearance may reveal an ongoing immersion in Catholic culture. Jerre Mangione refers to his Protestant uncle in both *Mount Allegro* and *An Ethnic at Large*. This uncle, Mangione writes, "was the only renegade" in the family, for he "was a non-conformist and a Baptist" (*Mount Allegro* 38). The Italian American who follows a Protestant path will be at least atypical, if not an outsider within a group of outsiders—a religious minority in an ethnic minority. Mangione describes this uncle humorously, if not endowing him with a touch of the buffoon. Luigi "was a celebrity among the relatives" (75–76) because of his conversion. Mangione says when Luigi first came to America he saw an Italian Baptist church and went inside where the minister greeted him kindly, Mangione recounts his uncle saying:

"It was the first happy face I had ever seen on a cleric [. . .] so I joined. We had a long talk first and he told me that you could go much further in this country if you weren't a Catholic. He said he had in his congregation some of the best-known Italian lawyers, doctors and politicians in town. The minister told me the truth. Did you ever hear of a Catholic who ever became President of the United States? Of course, I can't say that being a Baptist has got me anywhere in particular; but it is better than fussing over a lot of saints." (*Mount Allegro* 76)

Here we see the oft-repeated paradox that one becomes a nonconformist in the immigrant community so that one may better conform to the adoptive community.

Perhaps one of the reasons for Luigi's limited rise in America is the fact that he failed to attain proficiency in English. As Mangione puts it: "My Uncle Luigi, more than any other of my relatives, had to depend on his smiles and charms to maintain good relations with Americans. His English was so rudimentary that it could be understood only by Sicilians" (*Mount Allegro* 57). And his relatives kidded him about his attempts to sway them from their faith. "Whenever he ranted against Catholicism," Mangione writes, "my mother would smile patiently and tell him that he should certainly have become a priest instead of a mason" (*Mount Allegro* 79). Uncle Luigi, then, becomes a comic figure in the author's writing just as he was for the elders in his Rochester, New York, immigrant family.

The depiction of Italian American Protestants in Mario Puzo's *The Fortunate Pilgrim* and Helen Barolini's *Umbertina* expresses strong disparagement of Protestant characters. Chapter 6 of Puzo's novel almost entirely follows the interaction of Italian American Protestants and a recent convert, Frank Corbo, the husband of protagonist Lucia Santa. Are these fictive depictions critical because the authors are Catholic, because fiction necessitates a villain, or because as Lucia Santa believes, "Life was unlucky, you followed a new path at your peril. You put yourself at the mercy of fate" (12–13). In other words, even if, like Lucia, you never went to Mass and had no use for priests, some believe that it is better to stick with the devil you know.

Although Lucia Santa distrusts and dislikes the Protestant Coluccis from the moment she first meets them, she does not object to her husband's association with them for two reasons. Puzo writes, "She gave not her assent, for that was not hers to give; the father could not be vetoed. She gave her blessing" (94). And besides—and more importantly—Mr. Colucci promised Frank a job at Runkel's chocolate factory.

This section of *The Fortunate Pilgrim* also points to a connection between Protestantism and literacy. One of the tasks of missionaries in Italy had been the distribution of Bibles. Similarly in the New York of Puzo's story, Frank "took a red-edged holy book from the pocket of his jacket" and then bemoaned, "'This book has the truth and I can't even read it. It's in Italian and still I cannot read it'" (91). Mr. Colucci, however, "promised he would teach Frank Corbo to read and write. They would use the Bible as text" (94).

Lucia Santa's eyes are ours here; we see the scene from her perspective. Although these deeply religious missionaries have wrought "miracles"—"drunkards became total abstainers, evil men who regularly tattooed their wives and children black and blue became sweet as saints" (95)—"Lucia Santa raised her eyebrows in polite astonishment" (thus mocking Rev. Colucci's claim) (95). And although everyone in the room is "Italian," she sees differences between her family and the Coluccis: in class, in origin, and in language, as well as in religion. Lucia typifies the in-name-only Catholic that Protestants—both immigrant and native and both in the United States and in Italy—thought necessitated conversion to a living spirituality, at least from their Protestant perspective. Puzo writes that Lucia "had long ceased to think of God except to automatically curse his name for some misfortune" (96).

It is misfortune (not prosperity or renewal) that the Coluccis and their Literal Baptist Church bring to Lucia Santa and family. Frank soon sinks into the abyss of an extreme Protestant melancholy. Italian American converts followed a classic conversion process. Many of the autobiographies, as we have seen, record a standard path of sin and self-abasement, recognition and self-examination, testimony and sanctification. Luigi Turco recounts in his autobiography how he hungered "for a better moral and spiritual life" ("Brief Story" 3). The young Turco tired of his life, as Lewis Turco puts it regarding his father, as "a young hedonist" ("Father and Son" 34). But the desire for a rebirth had at first, Luigi notes, "created in me a melancholic attitude; the spirit of despair!" ("Brief Story" 3). Some spiritual pilgrims lose their way and remain stuck in this conversion stage, suffering Protestant melancholia. So it happened with Frank Corbo.

"Every night," Puzo narrates, Frank "went to the Coluccis' for reading lessons and then to the chapel for services and more lessons" (100). All goes well for a while, but Frank's favorite Bible verses are those "in which man was brought to book by a wrathful and revengeful God" (100). Frank begins to change. He does not eat. He stares at the ceiling. He rarely sleeps and when he does "he would wake in the middle of the night and curse his wife, first in a slow, then a quickening, rhythm—the rhythms of the Bible" (102). Frank Corbo declines into madness and a permanent institutionalization at Bellevue Hospital and then Pilgrim State Hospital for the Insane. Lucia Santa thinks of Colucci: "Callow, criminal in his meddlesome religiosity—he was the cause of her husband's illness" (105).

Even worse, even more villainous than the Coluccis are the Giordanis of Helen Barolini's *Umbertina*. Anna Giordani, a nurse—social worker among the Italians, comes from a northern Italian Waldensian background. She has some money and education. In other words, Anna and the main character Umbertina have little in common. Like Anna Ruddy or Mr. Colucci, it seems Anna's intentions are honorable, even if the benefits are arguable. Read to the end of the novel, read those final two pages of chapter 33 when Tina, the great-granddaughter, unknowingly sees Umbertina's beautiful *coperta*, wedding bedspread, at the Ellis Island Museum in an exhibit of artifacts from the Anna Giordani Collection (407). Umbertina sold this blanket to Anna in order to finance the family's move out of their decrepit life in tenement New York. Anna said she had arranged for a Quaker woman to buy the *coperta*, and when Umbertina has a change of fortune and wants to buy back the bedspread, Anna calls her an " 'Indian giver.' " Umbertina replies, " 'What have I to do with Indians?' " (77), but she might as well have been Chippewa as Calabrian because Umbertina, the narrative proves, was correct when she "wondered why this woman, who felt so superior because she was English-speaking and Protestant, still bothered to call herself Italian" (74). This Protestant missionary steals Umbertina's past and with it, a piece of her identity. Although this realization at the end of the saga both saddens and surprises the reader, Umbertina's message seems to reach Tina, her great-granddaughter. The *coperta* on display, Barolini says, spoke to Tina: "Of Italy and the past and keeping it all together for the future" (408).

Like Tina, I also seek "the past" as a way to keep "it all together for the future." Have I discovered my great-grandfather in a still-standing storefront along Congress Avenue in New Haven, a building that he once owned and where the *Alpha and Omega Assembly Newsletter* originated? Have I discovered him (or myself or you) in a photograph of a congregation in Monson, Massachusetts? Have I discovered him in these pages?

Alfredo Barone had a brother who also came to America, who also converted to the Baptist faith, and who also preached in the United States. Giovanni, or John, Barone settled in Waterbury, Connecticut. Angelo di Domenica mentions him once in his autobiography (*Protestant Witness* 55). I remember my father saying that John became a banker. Is this the actual American story? Alfredo wore the dark traditional clothes his entire life. Did John adopt the flannels of American business? I have one book that my great-grandfather gave to my grandfather. Alfredo gave it to his son twice. He gave it to Melchisedec in Calitri, Italy, on the occasion of his fourth birthday in 1897. Alfredo kept this book and gave it to his son again in May 1950, shortly before he died. Inside the volume are two inscriptions. The latter reads: "Conservato per mio figlio il Dr. Barone da me suo Padre per più di 50 anni" ("Saved for my son Dr. Barone by me his father for more than 50 years"). The book is *Gli Aninali Della Bibbia e le Lezioni Che Ci Danno* (*Bible Animals and Lessons Taught by Them*) by Richard Newton and translated by Giovanni Luzzi. Luzzi, a Protestant, preached in both the United States and Italy and wrote a history of Italian Protestantism. Newton wrote many books in the late nineteenth century of what might be called popular religion, for example, *Bible Models Or the Shining Lights of Scripture: A Book for Every Home* and *Five-Minute Talks for Young People; or, The Way to Success*. What is the relation between the late-nineteenth-century awakenings in Italy and in the United States, and what is the relation of these awakenings to the social gospel typified by Charles Sheldon (*In His Steps* 1896) and the commercial gospel of Bruce Barton (*The Man Nobody Knows* 1925)? Madison Grant in his anti-immigrant ranting proclaimed: "These immigrants adopt the language of the native American; they wear his clothes, they steal his name; and they are beginning to take his women, but they seldom adopt his religion or understand his ideals [. . .]" (81).

The history of Italian American Protestants in the early twentieth century shows that they did indeed do all of these things, though one might be reluctant to say Luigi Turco "stole" an Anglo girl. Yes, they might have changed Giovanni to John or they might have retained an

Italian name and mode of dress, but they also profoundly understood Protestantism, American ideals, and struggled to match that understanding to challenges both behind them in the home country and those still to come in their adopted land.

Chapter 2

To Struggle for a Place at the Table

In 1985 my wife and I went to London after I received a grant from the Pennsylvania Council on the Arts. While there we went to the British Library to look at Alfredo Barone's 1895 book, *La vita di Gesù Cristo ossia l'armonia degli evangeli* (*The Life of Jesus Christ or the Harmony of the Gospels*). At the Van Pelt Library, University of Pennsylvania, I had looked for it in the multivolume hard copy catalogs for the Library of Congress and the British Library. As soon as we got to the great domed reading room of the latter, an architectural gem designed by a Neapolitan exile, Antonio Panizzi, I completed a call slip and then we waited. The library assistant returned with disappointing news. On the call slip was the word: *mis-shelved*. We moved to Connecticut the following year and a few years later I wrote to the British Library and asked to purchase a photocopy of the book. Some months went by before I received a reply informing me that now the book appears to be "missing." In 2008 I tried again. This time I checked the British Library website and sent an e-mail message to the appropriate office. This time I asked for a CD scan. Soon I received a reply. The cost for electronic reproduction was expensive, but not prohibitive. I completed an official order request. On July 17, 2008 I received the following e-mail message: "Unfortunately we are not able to process your order as the item has been destroyed, for order number 08W02654P therefore your order has been cancelled." I wrote back right away and asked, "Why would such an item have been destroyed?" And moments later the Customer Services, Account Enquiries associate informed me that *La vita di Gesù Cristo ossia l'armonia degli evangeli* was among the many books "destroyed in the war." Some weeks later it occurred to me to check Italian libraries. Through the database known as WorldCat, I discovered two copies in central Italy: one in Florence and one in Rome. Again, I sent an e-mail message, in both English and Italian this time, inquiring about purchasing a CD scan, but I did not receive a reply.

At about this time, Stefano Luconi and I agreed to coedit the proceedings of the 2008 meeting of the American Italian Historical Association (now known as the Italian American Studies Association). After waiting a bit longer to see if I would receive a reply from Rome, I decided to ask Professor Luconi, who teaches in Rome and lives in Florence, if he could lend assistance. Kindly, he handled the whole operation for me and within two weeks I had *La vita di Gesù Cristo* on CD. Excitedly, I put the CD in my computer as soon as I received it and my first discovery: Alfredo Barone dedicated the volume to Rev. Robert Walker.

Rev. Walker served thirteen years in Naples as minister for the English Baptist Mission. At the end of the nineteenth century, the American mission board took over the work of the English Baptist Mission Society in southern Italy. Perhaps, that explains how Rev. Walker later became superintendent of Italian missions of the New York City Baptist Mission Society.

Alfredo Barone, like his mentor Rev. Walker, also came to the United States. A story from the April 1924 issue of *Missions: American Baptist Magazine* tells of a young Italian boy in Haverhill, Massachusetts, very much surprised "one Sunday afternoon [. . .] when he saw a man speaking to a little group of people in front of a store building that was being utilized as a mission" (212). Alfredo Barone was the preacher and this so shocked the boy for he had last seen Barone near San Sossio, Italy. The boy, Francesco, "Had been the first to raise the cry of 'Protestant,'" when the representative of the Baptist Mission Society of London approached San Sossio.

> The street became crowded with people. The antagonisms born of their traditions, combined with actual terror, transformed these peace-loving townspeople into a mob. A shower of stones fell about the stranger. (Hayne 210)

The author of this narrative relates that: "The event was but one of a series of persecutions which he [Barone] had been experiencing" (Hayne 210).

The persecutions a minister such as Barone encountered came at the hands of others than countryside Catholic youths and townspeople. If Catholics rejected Italian Protestant ministers for being irreligious, liberals of the new nation's political structure rejected them for being too religious, and English and American Protestants rejected them for being too Italian. As one English Baptist complained: "the fixing of a native preacher who invariably becomes a kind of spiritual sicknurse, is the cause of much missionary failure and pauperizes *souls* and degrades our social and socializing faculties" ("Untitled Repudiation" 2).

During the final decades of the nineteenth century, Protestantism offered an alternative religious experience to Catholicism for some Italians, either in Italy or in America shortly after emigration. Though living in a period of some support for Protestant faiths from political leaders as well as living soon after the defeat of the Papal military, these Italian Protestants struggled against the vigorous and at times violent residual strength of the Catholic Church and its pervasive influence on the populace at large. The Italian Protestants also struggled against a new secular strain in elite society and, perhaps paradoxically, against the hierarchy and condescension of Protestant missionaries. For example, the longtime leading American Baptist in Rome, Rev. George Boardman Taylor, wrote in 1890: "We had first the meeting of the Baptist Union and then that of our own evangelists. I was made president of both as well as of the Executive Committee. No sinecure I assure you, as in some respects it would be easier to preside over the S.B.C. [Southern Baptist Convention—with a vastly larger membership] than over these twenty-five or thirty Italians" (*Life and Letters* 274). As noted previously, Alfredo Barone dedicated his 1895 book to "Rev. Roberto Walker, *mio caro sopraintendente*" ("my dear superintendent").

In addition to this religious colonialism, Italian Protestant preachers faced the threat of physical harm to themselves or members of their congregations. For example, the 1902 Italian Baptist Mission Board Report noted that at Tufo, "the wife of one of the brethren had her hair torn from her head when it was known that she had accepted the Gospel." Rev. Antonio Arrighi described in his memoir the difficulties he had in Florence securing a place to hold services. Often a mere *locale* (small storefront or room) functioned as a chapel, but usually only after an intense struggle to locate one that could be rented. Despite the persecutions and difficulties, despite their many hardships, despite "the tomb like chilliness of the *locale*," as one American preacher described it (Edward Judson "Foreword" to Taylor *Life and Letters*), the Italian Protestant preachers persevered to create a yearned-for sacred place.

In the period of nation-building and national unification, many contested the place of religion in the formation of a new consciousness. The establishment of first an independent, then a large unified Italy required the victory of nationalistic forces in the Papal States. The complexity of religious and political life can be seen in the somewhat contrasting conclusions of two recent monographs. Whereas Peter R. D'Agostino in *Rome in America* argues that Church and state opposed one another in a hostile and antagonistic relationship, Mark I. Choate argues that there was some cooperation between Church and state to create an Italian nation at home by creating Italians abroad: "Though bitter enemies at home, the Catholic Church and Italian state were able to work together to 'make Italians,' and Catholics, in emigrant colonies abroad" (145).

Rev. Taylor ended his book on Italy with a chapter titled "The Evangelization of Italy." He argued that no Italians could be created for the recently formed nation without an extensive religious awakening. (This is somewhat similar to his colleagues working with Italians in the United States who believed that there could be "no Americanization without Evangelization" [*Report of the Committee on Americanization* 20].) "To the political movements which prepared the revolution," Taylor wrote, "corresponded a religious movement limited, but spontaneous, weak, but genuine" (379). Later, he lamented:

> It must be admitted that after the first novelty had worn away, the car of evangelization in Italy did not move forward so rapidly as many had hoped, nay, that its wheels sometimes seemed to drag heavily. Some who had professed conversion and united with the churches in the excitement of unwonted political freedom fell away, having really confounded evangelical churches with political societies, and mistaken their joy in civil liberty for a religious experience. (412)

Confounded were these relationships, even within Rev. Taylor's text and if the web of complexity remains difficult to pull into a tight narrative line, let us sketch here the Italian preacher's situation.

Giovanni Luzzi, one of the most prominent Protestant preachers and thinkers in Italy at that time, once rhetorically asked how the revival in religion came about; his reply: "Nobody can say exactly" ("Three Romantic Chapters" 291). Indeed, many occurrences on the peninsula seemed to be instances of the mysterious workings of God. "Two men, for instance," Luzzi wrote, "went one day to take a bath in the Arno near Signa. They saw a book being carried away by the current; one of them caught hold of it and found that it was a Bible. He began to read and study it and in a short time was led to the truth as it is in Christ" ("Three Romantic Chapters" 292).

Antonio Mangano, an Italian American Baptist, stated the purpose and origin of religious revivalism in Italy with more matter-of-fact concision and precision than Luzzi's linguistic shrug of the shoulders. Mangano stated: "Evangelization is the chief business of the Protestant church in Italy" (*Sons of Italy* 87). Whereas Luzzi claimed the religious revival began in the early nineteenth century, commensurate with renewals in literature and science, Mangano said: "The Protestant propaganda in Italy as a whole began in 1870 when the temporal power of the Pope came to an end and the soldiers of Victor Emmanuel entered the Eternal City through the breach in the ancient walls of Rome" (*Sons of Italy* 87).

The American Union Church in Florence became an early advocate of evangelization. The Annual Report for 1869 recalled that "services in Florence for the benefit of travelers and residents were commenced [. . .] in the year 1861" (3). Three works soon became the church mission: a new chapel ("that can accommodate with ease two hundred persons" [Annual Report for 1868]), the Evangelical Schools ("the number of pupils enrolled is not far from 300, making them the largest Protestant institution in Italy" [Annual Report for 1868]), and an orphan Asylum. Most evangelical efforts placed emphasis on children and Italy's future. "We are led to conclude that the most inviting field for evangelical effort is amongst the children, and if Italy is to be truly regenerated, we should begin at the foundation of the social structure and elevate the young mind" (Annual Report for 1869). The 1869 Report noted that these charitable institutions had been under Signor Ferretti's guidance. No Americans, the Report asserted, "have assumed any responsibilities in reference to these charities." However, Americans did receive and disburse all funds. Despite the fact that Salvatore Ferretti "has long been a faithful evangelist and has suffered in the Saviour's cause," his name did not appear in the Report as an officer of the church.

he yearly Baptist Mission Reports (1906) Rev. Ever- he following passionate reason for evangelization: "A ival in Italy would shake the nations—it would be a a miracle is possible with God." Although optimism and diction sometimes became inflated, the hard facts were the numbers of conversions always remained pitifully small. The Italian American Episcopal priest, Enrico Sartorio, wrote in 1918: "No matter how doubtful the religious future of Italy may be, one thing is certain: Italy will never become Protestant. [. . .] No matter to how great an extent Italians may become anti-clericals they are not at all anti-Catholics; the dream of making Italy a Presbyterian, a Methodist, or a Unitarian country will always remain a dream" (98–99). The Baptist reverend George Boardman Taylor had more hope for the Protestant evangelization of Italy, but, nonetheless, his 1900 Report noted that in Naples, a city of 700,000, there were but 114 Baptists. Ironically, a section titled the "Power of the Gospel" soon follows in this Report. Also, many of the converted left Italy for America, and so missionaries felt somewhat ambivalent about how they often secured converts only to lose them "to America, the Italians' paradise" (Baptist Mission Report 1907). Yet, when in America these converts often supported missions back home in Italy; for example, converts from Calitri who emigrated sent money back to Italy for a church building in their native town (Report 1906). Rev. Antonio Roca of Hartford, Connecticut saw some of his baptized return to Italy where they established a Baptist church in the southern hill town of Bisaccia ("Home Mission Work" 43).

Beside the low number of congregants, these missions and missionaries were ever beset by financial worry. Rev. Walker wrote frequently to London regarding funds, both personal salary and institutional support (Letters). Taylor, too, wrote his board in America with similar concerns. In April 1874, he wrote: "The Board seems embarrassed, and I have been keeping the mission going by borrowing constantly. You can imagine the disagreeableness of this as well as the anxiety I am kept in" (*Life and Letters* 190).

Taylor believed that "Italy with the gospel would be one of the best and happiest, as she already is the fairest, of earth's lands" (*Italy* viii). In March of 1873 the Foreign Mission Board of the Southern Baptist Convention appointed the Virginian Taylor to lead evangelization in Rome.

> The practical sagacity, the broad cultivation, the elevated character, and missionary spirit of this brother, render him, in the opinion of the Board, eminently qualified for succession to the troubled things at Rome, for training native preachers, and undisciplined churches, and for pressing forward the work of the Lord by the pulpit and the press, and by his personal consecration to the holy cause. (*Life and Letters* 164)

He remained in this work for the remainder of his life, more than thirty years. He often exercised his wisdom, wit, kindness, and intelligence. One of his sons noted: "he loved Rome and Romans, and mankind generally, and was deeply interested in all phases of human life" (*Life and Letters* 206). Yet, he was never free from prejudice and all error that followed from it.

He first went to Italy in 1870. "I was only a summer tourist," he wrote, "and had no idea of spending a quarter of a century in Italy than I now have of a flight to the moon" (*Italy* 113). On a few occasions the well-read Taylor had some correspondence with Mark Twain, and Taylor sometimes mimics a novelist's narrative and poetic skills. Regarding his first night in Italy, Taylor recalled: "I seemed to be in fairyland, and the feeling was only increased when a few hours later I was supping at Arona, in an arbor illumined by the moon and by Chinese lanterns hung among the foliage of the trees" (*Italy* 113).

Taylor viewed his early years of evangelization in Italy as a volatile era. "The new liberty," he wrote, "opened the way to abuses. On the streets of Rome sheets ridiculing priests, bishops, cardinals, and the pope himself, were posted and sold; science was deified, and atheism showed a bold front, while in the schools anti-Christian teaching had its way" (*Italy* 72–73). The same freedom that permitted the above named abuses, also opened wide the door, as he put it, "for the antidote in the preaching of the gospel" (73).

Yet, it was no easy task to pass through the wide open door; the antidote proved to be medicine hard to take. Many were persecuted by the Catholic Church, by their fellow townspeople, and by family members. Such persecution occurred across the length of the peninsula, from north to south. Taylor told of a purchase early in the religious awakening of a vacant Catholic church in Genoa by the Waldensians.

The church had even served as a stable before this transfer. However, Taylor wrote, "as soon as it was proposed to use it for evangelical worship and preaching of the gospel, the Roman Catholic party raised such an uproar, and brought such influence to bear upon the authorities, that the building had to be resold" (*Italy* 389–390). Arrighi stated regarding his return to Italy from America to preach the evangelical gospel: "Although Florence has been regarded as the most intelligent of all Italian cities, yet I had hard work to rent a house for the purpose. Finally I had to go outside the city walls to secure such a place. This shows that even among some who regard themselves as highly cultured, superstition and bigotry are to be found" (254–255). When Arrighi did secure a building to use as a chapel, various protests followed, including a "mob sent there to do me harm," as he recalled, "or to take my life. They howled and shouted, 'Down with the heretic!' " (260).

In Rev. Landells's critical remarks on English Baptist missionary work in Italy he noted that Rev. Walker had great difficulty finding a permanent home for the evangelical work. Walker had been using part of a Presbyterian church in Naples. Landells wrote, "I told him plainly I did not think it likely to succeed" ("Remarks"). However, the English Baptist under Walker's guidance did attempt to construct a complete religious compound on the Via Foria, not far from the Botanical Gardens. Walker's sketch for the complex shows a garden, a chapel, a schoolroom, three halls, a house, an apartment, and bathrooms ("Letter with plan"). Landells complained that the property was "not in the best part of the city for our purpose." No matter, he added, "negotiations for this purpose were, through the influence of the priests, thwarted again and again just as they were nearing completion" ("Remarks").

Small towns were as inhospitable as big cities. Taylor noted that, "often when the gospel is first preached in a secondary town, the pulpits of the papal churches resound with the cry, 'Death to the Protestants!' " (*Italy* 402) and the Baptist Mission Report of 1907 noted that two small towns suffered greatly from an eruption of Vesuvius that the Catholics claimed Baptists had caused by their preaching and, at the same time, the Baptists thought the Catholics "foolish when they carried about in processions wooden images of the Virgin and saints, hoping thereby to hinder the flow of the hot lava and to stop the earthquakes."

Persecutions were sometimes quite violent. Taylor wrote, "On the evening of May 7, 1871, when the locale of the Wesleyan congregation was crowded, a bomb was exploded which broke all the glass in the windows and put out the lights, but did no other damage" (*Italy* 408). The Mission Reports describe acts of violence every year. One report (1908) noted quite simply, "In this city [Bari] evangelicals have been killed for their faith." According to this report the conversion of a priest in Lioni led to the converted fleeing from home. His father disinherited him and pledged to kill him should he return. It was never easy to convert. The 1900 report described "the wife of a baker," who for more than three years "remained firm [in her conversion] despite beatings received from her blaspheming husband, who also more than once drove her out of the house, forbidding her to return." Eventually, her perseverance in the face of such persecution paid off when her husband, too, converted.

A common and shared belief held by many of the American and English missionaries, to use the plea of one Baptist report (1906), was that, "Our greatest need in Italy is a number of truly consecrated natives to preach the gospel." Yet, so often the missionary leaders acted like colonizers of the soul, *padroni* (bosses) for the faith of others. Remember, one reason the Baptist Foreign Mission Board sent Rev. Taylor to Rome was so that he might tame the "undisciplined" churches (*Life and Letters* 164).

In "The Evangelization of Italy," the final chapter of *Italy and the Italians*, Taylor regretted that "the most honest mistakes were made in those earliest years in receiving members and in putting men into the ministry, so that many in both proved to be unworthy" (412). Late in his Italian career Taylor and his colleagues opened a theological school in Rome. The 1907 report counted ten students, two Wesleyans, one "found wanting" and dismissed and "another, who studied with us for two years and cost us no little, shamefully forsook our work and went to South America to enter business." The director, D. G. Whittinghill and the rest of the faculty (three Americans and one Italian) prayed "that God will not punish him according to his merits."

Taylor's son, George Braxton, observed in the *Life and Letters* that his father spent much of his time "answering multitudinous letters in Italian, and many of them disagreeable and annoying [. . .]." George Braxton Taylor then provides an extract from a letter written by Taylor senior regarding this tedious state of affairs:

> I remember that I spoke of my habit of replying, even to the most offensive letters from our evangelists, with delicacy and with Christian charity, but it is quite necessary

to complete the statement by saying that this is not done without a struggle. (282)

The Italian evangelists suffered persecution from their fellow Italians and condescension from their Anglo colleagues.

Arrighi sensed that Anglo missionaries would have neither full understanding of nor deep appreciation for contemporary Italians. They might admire Botticelli and Dante, as Taylor did, but even though they devoted much of their lives to missionary work in Italy, such foreign men might miss something essential in the current moment of the relatively new nation and its people. Therefore, Arrighi, a former drummer boy for Garibaldi, and a prisoner of war who escaped to America and converted in Iowa, on completion of his studies at Boston Theological Seminary, had an "intense longing to go there as the herald of a free salvation" (231). He added:

> It was my desire to work in connection with a native church, for I have always been of the opinion that such a church would be more successful in evangelizing the Italians than an imported one under the control of an imported superintendent. No one can understand the Italian character as well as an Italian. (231–232)

It was one such imported superintendent to whom Alfredo Barone dedicated his study of the harmony of the Gospels. Barone usually referred to himself as the Rev. Alfredo Barone and later as Rev. Dr. Barone, but in issues of the *Baptist Home Mission Monthly* and other such publications editors or authors call him either Mr. Barone or Pastor Barone, as if knowledge, honor, and respect must be reserved for New Englanders and Virginians. That young man, Francesco Sannella, who threw stones at Alfredo Barone in Italy, and then saw him again in Haverhill, Massachusetts, became known as "Frank" and followed Barone in the position of pastor at the Italian Baptist Church in Monson. As the editors noted in the November 1908 issue of the *Baptist Home Mission Monthly*:

> Mr. Sannella is one of our most gifted and trusted men. The story of his conversion is most interesting. Some eight years ago when Mr. Barone began his work among the Ital-

ians at Haverhill, Frank Sannella as a boy was working in a shoe factory and helping to care for his brothers and sisters who were largely dependent upon him. When Mr. Barone was preaching in the open air, Frank stood on the edge of the crowd and threw stones at the missionary [as he had in San Sossio]. Finally the Spirit of God touched his heart and he became a most zealous convert to the faith. ("An Interesting Career" 449)

Within the immigration push-pull paradigm, Italians have epitomized those pushed from their old country rather than pulled to a new one. And yet economic disaster, fear of conscription, high taxation, and drought may not fully explain every individual's experience. Perhaps for a few, those American national virtues honored in innocent grade-school Thanksgiving-time pageants have some merit. Yes, the Episcopalian Enrico Sartorio wrote in 1918: "Looking facts in the face, Italians are not imitators of the Puritans, who came to America to find political and religious freedom. They came for bread and butter" (16). And yet, perhaps America pulled one man from the hill towns northeast of Naples to evangelize among those pushed out of those very same towns. Men converted by Alfredo Barone in one such town and who settled in Monson, Massachusetts, to work in the local quarry issued a heartfelt plea to Baptist officials for the inspiration of their former missionary pastor (at that time ministering to Italians in Haverhill and Springfield, having arrived in New York in 1899). Barone answered that call in 1903, and by the following year the Westfield Baptist Association recognized and received the Italian Baptist Association of Monson into fellowship (Minutes 1904, 11). He continued his missionary work, preaching until his death in 1950. The two front steps of the Monson church can still be seen on Margaret Street, not too far from the entrance to the long-abandoned quarry.

Chapter 3

Does Christ Linger at Eboli?

A 1912 pamphlet from the Italian Baptist Church of Meriden, Connecticut, noted that Rev. Rolando Giuffrida "had delivered twenty-four lectures every year on American history and the privileges and duties of American citizenship" (*Notes from 1912 Pamphlet*). Curiously, the Protestant movement that grew out of the turbulence of the reunification years in Italy became a program to propel mostly Southern Italian immigrants into the mainstream of life in America. In Southern Italy, Protestantism resulted from many divisions within the nation, such as those in region and class and political perspective, whereas in the United States it acted as an agent for unity.

In this chapter I discuss the complexity and diversity of Italian Protestantism from the late nineteenth century to the early twentieth century in order to describe what conversion to Protestantism offered in Italy or in America and what effect it had in both theory and fact for immigrants in America. It argues that whereas Italian Protestantism was an alternative expression of faith and spirituality to the authoritarianism of Catholicism, in America Protestantism became for some, in addition to a means to negotiate two worlds, a conservative vehicle of nationalism and for assimilation. In closing, the chapter briefly explains the decline of Italian American Protestantism.

Protestantism originated partly in reaction to the exploitative authoritarianism of the Catholic Church, and out of the liberalizing trends of the Risorgimento such as its call to liberty and equality and the belief in freedom of religion and of the press—forces that led to and were a part of the reunification of Italy. Ever at odds were the authoritarianism of the Church and the idea of a national representative government. During the years after the unification, there was an increase in anti-Catholic sentiment among the peasant population. Many believed the Catholic clergy had more interest in protecting their social and economic privileges than in administering to the spiritual welfare of their congregations. In the intellectual sphere new knowledge in many fields led some to question what they saw as the backwardness of the Church, which even as late as 1907 condemned new modes of thought in the encyclical *Pascendi Dominici Gregis*. The Risorgimento can be thought of as a second Renaissance and not just a nationalist movement, as a time of new movements in the arts and the sciences as well as in politics. The Church, on the other hand, felt threatened by this new knowledge as well as by the political struggles that would unify a nation and along with that unification bring the vast papal territories into secular control. For example, prior to 1861, a number of political exiles from Italy lived elsewhere in Europe, especially in London, and, as I will explain in more detail later, diverse and fervent debate of ideas in these lands presented possibilities of all sort that differed from those available in the various divided states of pre-unified Italy. Later, at the end of the century and following, emigration to foreign lands had opened new horizons for mostly illiterate Italian peasants, especially in how they lived and how they worshiped. Even if immigrants lived in an Italian enclave, they still gained exposure in an American city and at an American workplace to new customs, and their children would learn new ways of being (often in conflict with those of their parents) at American schools. Furthermore, in America some immigrants may have attended a Protestant church, at least at first, due to proximity, and the fact that the nearest Catholic church did not welcome them or had no priest who spoke their language.

Yet, in addition to the Risorgimento, the reunification, conflict between church and state, exile and emigration, an important factor in the appeal of Protestantism for some must have been the divided nature of the unified state. What nobel laureate in literature Günter Grass (1990) said of the new Germany at the end of the twentieth century can be easily said (though for different reasons) about the new Italy at the end of the nineteenth century: two states—one nation? Did the leaders, documents, and institutions of unification prepare Italy for its future or build a foundation for crisis? One recent book, Pino Aprile's *Terroni* (2011, which has sold more than 200,000 copies in Italy) argues that at the time of unification in Southern Italy military commanders from the North engaged in a sort of Sherman's march to the sea, burning and destroying propetry everywhere they marched and massacring thousands. Aprile asserts that: "The impoverishment of the South, in order to increase the wealth of the North, was the reason for the Unification of Italy, not the consequence" (95). What Grass said of Germany is similar to what Aprile says of Italy, "There has never really been a Unification of Italy. It is not one country, but two" (222). In some ways, the reunification of Italy perpetuated old and created new bitter divisions and conflicts, ones which, in Aprile's view, continue today and may even get worse before they get better.

I take my title for this chapter from Carlo Levi's (1945) well-known memoir *Christ Stopped at Eboli* (*Cristo si è fermato a Eboli*). Levi writes about the impact of poverty on the people of the South and his experience during the Fascist era—in some respects well beyond the main focus of this chapter. And yet it is not geographically outside my bounds. Carlo Levi, born into a wealthy Jewish family in Turin, was a physician, artist, author, and political activist, arrested by Mussolini because of his anti-Fascist activities. Levi, sentenced to a year (1935–1936) of internal banishment and sent into exile to a remote mountain town (Aliano, Lucania) in a region of Southern Italy known as Basilicata, wrote his memoir about the profound hardships and poverty peasants of Aliano experienced on a daily basis. Near the start of his narrative of that year, he writes about the people who say of themselves:

> "We're not Christians," they say. "Christ stopped short of here, at Eboli." "Christian," in their way of speaking means "human being," and this almost proverbial phrase that I have often heard them repeat may be no more than the expression of a hopeless feeling of inferiority. We're not Christians, we're not human beings; we're not thought of as men but simply as beasts, beasts of burden, or even less than beasts, mere creatures of the wild. (3)

In effect, Levi gives voice to the people of this remote mountain town who feel they have been bypassed by Christianity because they are thought by the Catholic Church not to be fully human. Protestant evangeliation in the South, I believe, returns to some—through Christ and the Gospel—their humanity. This result, this belief is what I would like to suggest occurred for some in the South.

Radical labor leader Carlo Tresca linked an evangelical anti-Catholic Christianity with socialist labor activities. Tresca referred to early Socialism in Italy as "missionary work" (31) and noted that his journalism "exposed [. . .] the fallacy of the Catholic Church, considered by us socialists the bulwark of capitalism" (36). Furthermore, Marcella Bencivenni has recently observed that "there are distinct elements of continuity between [Arturo] Giovannitti's activity as a pastor and as a labor agitator: In both cases he saw himself as a sort of missionary, a prophet of the poor and the oppressed" (163). Levi suggested at the end of his work that equality would come to Italy only through a revolution by the agricultural workers of the South in unity with the industrial workers of the North. The evangelist offered a revolution in the individual spirit and conscience if not in the entire lumpenproletariat and political realm.

Antonio Gramsci was one of the foremost original Marxist philosophers and thinkers in the twentieth century and a founding member of the Communist Party of Italy. He died at age forty-six after twenty years of imprisonment in Rome. Born into a Roman Catholic family, he was an avowed atheist and his ashes are buried in the Protestant cemetery in Rome. He wrote his well-known notes on *The Southern Question* shortly before his imprisonment by Benito Mussolini's Fascist regime. For Gramsci, the Southern question cannot be separated from the Vatican question (20), and he claims that "the priest represents to the peasant" three things: "a land administrator," "a usurer," and "a man subject to all common passions" (38). Italian intellectuals (i.e., the upper- and middle-class intelligentsia), according to Gramsci, bind the Southerner to large landowners and "preserve the status quo" (40). In his popular book of 1902 historian Luigi Villari noted:

> The countless grotesque and degrading superstitions in which so many of the peasants still believe, are in many cases fostered by the priesthood, who hope by that means to retain their hold on the masses, and even the more educated and liberal-minded among them do little activity to combat such beliefs. (159)

The Roman Catholic Church, then, was vehemently antimodernist, not only in the sense of opposition to any reform movement from within the Church itself, but also in opposition to new and contemporary ideas in a wide range of fields. The Protestant evangelists, often university educated, were one group of intellectuals who challenged the political status-quo of the Catholic Church. The Protestant missionaries in the South during the late nineteenth century and early twentieth century may have blamed an entrenched Church and its priests for the impoverishment of the South, but they put more emphasis on change (conversion) than on blame. In other words, the Protestant convert in spiritual autobiography would say that inspiration gained in reading scripture played a more important role than did the shortcomings of contemporary Catholicism. Some of the Protestant preachers began their religious careers as Catholic priests. For example, F[rancis] C[lement] Capozzi graduated from the Roman seminary "De Propaganda Fide" ("Where I Found God" 1). He then secretly read the writings of the Catholic modernists "who felt that the time had arrived for adapting religion to the thought and life of the modern world" (1). He felt that if he ministered to immigrants in America "the claims of the mind might be silenced [. . .]" (2). But in America he discovers that Protestants are not villains, as he had been taught to believe, and as he read more religious writing than he had access to in Italy, his doubts continued and he came to the conclusion that "In the light of the Gospel democracy the ladder of the papal hierarchy appeared to me as rank paganism" (5). He asked himself, "Could there be any relationship between the thorny crown surrounding Christ's head and the Pope's jeweled tiara?" (8). He became an Episcopal priest who ministered to Pennsylvania congregations for more than thirty-five years.

Capozzi recalls with dismay that in 1851 Count Pietro Guicciardini was arrested for having been found reading the Bible (*Protestantism* 28). If an aristocrat faced such discipline, what then of the millions of illiterate *contadini*? Protestant faiths are word centered rather than ritual centered and encouragement of literacy, if nothing else or more than anything else, threatened the status quo of Southern Italy. And this is true for the high church "Catholic-Protestant" faith, the Episcopal Church, too. For example, even as late as his mission report of 1943, Father Paolo Vasquez of Hartford's Italian Episcopal church concluded: "St. Paul's stands here as a symbol of a true and fine catholic church [*sic*], preaching The Gospel of our Lord and trying to convert souls, ridding them from a false and superstitious doctrine which has been taught to them for many centuries" (5). Protestant evangelization in the South and in America returns to some, through Christ and the Gospel, their humanity.

In the South, however, an evangelist's challenges to the status quo could backfire, could be called by the Catholic Church explicitly political, and then result in the censoring or imprisonment of an evangelist (as we will see in the instance of Barone at Trevico). The examples could be supplemented with literally hundreds of others in addition to those cited in the previous chapter. The Church resorted to all sorts of questionable acts in an attempt to suppress Protestantism. Nor were conflicts easily resolved. Piedmont had granted some liberty of faith in 1848, and the Pope's temporal power came to an end with the incorporation of Rome and the papal lands into the new nation. Reform leader, Count Cavour, famously proclaimed, "Libera chiesa in libero stato" ("a free church in a free state"). Yet, the Pope and most leaders of the Catholic Church argued that temporal power had to be restored in order for spiritual power to have its fullest meaning for the faithful. Others saw this argument as nothing but an effort by the Church to consolidate its political hegemony over Italy. This "Roman question," as it has been called, lasted for a very long time and perhaps still exists for Italy today. (The debate continues, and I discuss this question more fully in chapter 4). For example, the Italian-born American Baptist Antonio Mangano observed in the early 1930s: "There are two influential papers published in New York City which are assisted financially by [the Catholic] church and [Italian] state to spread a propaganda that is pro Pope-pro Italy, often Anti-American, and always Anti-Protestant" ("The Closing of the Italian School" 5). In Italy, after decades of some religious tolerance, the Fascist state mandated in 1929 the exclusion of Protestantism and recognition of Catholicism as a state religion. Protestants faced renewed persecution. The 1948 constitution changed the Fascist mandate in theory but not in fact, and so separate non-Catholic faiths have worked for legal recognition in contemporary Italy. In 1994, for example, the Baptists secured their Agreement for Freedom of Worship in Italy.

In the nineteenth century, Catholic priests in Italy spoke of the Protestant devil and evangelists spoke of the papal darkness. The Protestants had some overlap with state power in that unification leaders spoke of an end to foreign and domestic tyranny, and by the latter Garibaldi and other leaders of the Risorgimemto always meant the Catholic Church. Always propagandist for reform and nationalism linked political and moral emancipation. The moral or spiritual movement opposed the oppression and tyranny of the Catholic Church and the political movement opposed the oppression and tyranny of foreign rule, and so these movements linked in anti-Catholicism and a belief in opposition to tyranny and support for various freedoms.

Giovanni Luzzi, professor in the Waldensian Theological Seminary at Florence, delivered a series of lectures at Princeton Theological Seminary during the academic year of 1912–1913. In his lecture on the Italian advocates of reform and unification who lived in exile during the mid-nineteenth century, Luzzi noted that for Gabriele Rossetti ("the bard of the Neapolitan revolution" of 1820), "his ideal" "was at one time a political and religious one" (*The Struggle for Christian Truth* 257, 263). Again, the belief these exiles held was that, on the one hand, there were those who advocated political and religious freedom and, on the other hand, there were those who perpetuated age-old forms of tyranny and oppression. Rossetti, a Neapolitan Italian poet and scholar, was forced into political exile in 1821 for support of Italian revolutionary nationalism. Many of his published poems were patriotic and also supported the popular movement in Southern Italy. He became professor of Italian at King's College in London.

Also in London, Luzzi added, Giuseppe Mazzini (1805–1872), one of the leading revolutionary activists for the unification of Italy, and Filippo Pistrucci (an Italian artist and poet) organized the Italian Free School in 1841. "Pistrucci represented the evangelical idea; Mazzini the political, because Mazzini never could conceive the two as separated from each other" (Luzzi, *The Struggle for Christian Truth* 275). Luzzi concluded that all the Risorgimento leaders-in-exile had "an ardent desire to see, some time or other, the Vatican crushed [. . .]" (285). In sum, the reformers and evangelists linked political emancipation with moral emancipation. As Luigi Settembrini, man of letters and politician wrote in a letter from 1864: "Political without religious freedom is nothing but a short-lived fire, and cannot last" (Luzzi 302).

A more recent historian of Italian Protestantism in his book *Risorgimento e protestanti* (1989) ("Protestants and the Risorgimento") points to "new knowledge" as well as Italians experiencing life abroad in other European nations as an important influence on both political and spiritual change. For example, he observes that Giovan Francesco Salvemini (1704–1791), a Tuscan who converted to Protestantism in Switzerland, had the door of faith opened by his learning Newtonian science ["Anche per lui la porta della fede fu la nuova scienza newtoniana"] (38).

New science, new faith, new politics often went together in Protestantism, whereas "the Pope," according to Luzzi, "was an avowed enemy of all progress; he refused to admit railways, telegraphs, and scientific congresses in his States" (*The Struggle for Christian Truth* 252). A story from an early-twentieth-century Protestant missionary tract (1914) makes these connections between science and religion very clear. Eugenio, a young Piedmontese man, studies agricultural science soon after he inherits a tract of land and at the same time that he converts to Protestantism. Eugenio applies new scientific techniques to grow his crops. The local priest "'says that Signor Eugenio is a religious revolutionist, and it would seem that he is not content with changing our religion: he actually wishes to change our ideas of the land!'" (Anderson 36). The author continues:

> But before many seasons had passed, the most antiquated and bitter enemies of progress were glad to learn and adopt the agricultural methods introduced by Eugenio, and in consequence the whole district became prosperous. Many land owners sent their peasants to his fields to study the new means of receiving richer returns from the soil. While Eugenio freely and gladly offered to all the benefits of his agricultural studies, he quite as freely and still more gladly made known to them the good news of salvation. This, however, increased the opposition of the priests, and the young heretical landowner was now engaged in a daily battle with papal Rome. (37)

Science and religion have been linked in this passage, and clearly Protestantism and Catholicism are in conflict. Another division remains apparent but not accentuated or commented on by the author: the conflict between landowners and laborers. Such divisions—both those that are very apparent and those less apparent—emigrants carried with them in their cultural baggage.

The decade of the 1890s during which mass emigration begins to take place from the south is also the decade of extensive Protestant evangelization in the south. The Baptist Mission Report of 1905 speaks of "the loss by emigration" from this region. The Report notes that "One church—Miglionico—has 27 members in America," and adds that "with such yearly losses, it becomes very difficult to increase our membership." Then, in addition to emigration, the Report notes other challenges to evangelization along North–South division lines: "In Southern Italy the greatest obstacles are filth, poverty, ignorance, superstition and persecution; while in the North our greatest foes are Atheistic Socialism and religious indifference." Perhaps in the North evangelists approached a more affluent audience than the agricultural workers they addressed in the South—though Rev. Whittinghill said all Italian Baptist church members were "poor, some very poor [. . .]" ("The Italian Mission" 154). The American Baptists who evangelized in Italy—all across the peninsula—always divided yearly Mission Reports into North and South: *Two States—One Nation*? At any rate, all these divisions went to America with emigrants.

Additionally, in America similar problems of migration and numbers confronted preachers. In the United States, immigrants often moved for employment and eventually when Italian colonies—rural, small town, and urban—dissipated, Italians who had converted to a Protestant faith (and their children) usually entered an "American" church.

~

During the reunification years, religion and politics often became conflated, and yet Protestant missionaries often struggled to maintain a distinct boundary between the two spheres. Meanwhile in America, many Italian Protestant ministers turned both overtly political and more conservative. In the Old World, the ministers offered an alternative religious experience to Catholicism and an experience that emphasized the necessity of literacy so that one could read the Bible for oneself—experiences that challenged the dominant order of things—whereas in the New World some worked diligently to move themselves and those to whom they ministered into the dominant culture (though a different dominant culture than that which existed in Italy). A phrase like "there is no Americanization without Evangelization" (*Report of the Committee* 20) accentuates this fact. Hence, in the pamphlet from 1912 the Meriden Church in Connecticut asks the rhetorical question, "Do Italians converts make good American citizens?" And the reply: "Yes! If they are good Christians [i.e., Protestants]. For a good Christian [Protestant] will be a good citizen."

Consider the fact that Antonio Mangano in his student commencement address for the Brown University class of 1899 stated:

"the peoples of our new dependencies cannot leap in a single day from absolute barbarism to the most perfect Anglo-Saxon civilization: but that does not in the least excuse us from granting to them every opportunity for development" (8). American civilization, for this young Italian-born Brown graduate, formed the finest in world culture, and this way of life had to be Anglo-Saxon and Protestant. And so when he wrote about evangelizing Italian immigrants to America in 1917, he said: "When the message of Christ is presented in all its simplicty and power and the moral side of religion is given emphasis and prominence, the Italian, whether a zealous Catholic or no, says: 'Yes, you are right, that is true'" (*Religious Work Among Italians* 23), as well he should if he seeks to become an "American," or so these Protestant preachers believed and repeatedly stated. This America of immigrants from Italy and elsewhere in Southern and Eastern Europe is not the country of Will Herberg's mid-fifties Protestant-Catholic-Jew or today's ecumenical, postethnic, and postracial America. This is a time and a place that forcefully and repeatedly defined itself as strictly Protestant.

To quote from the Italian-born Baptist minister Angelo di Domenica: "If we desire to bring the Italians into the realm of true Americanism we must give them the Gospel" ("The Sons of Italy" 191). Di Domenica believed that at most only 10 percent of the Italians in America attended Catholic services, and he asserted that "for centuries the Italians have been oppressed by the papal system which has retarded the development of their economic, political, social and educational life" ("The Sons of Italy" 190). Indifference and oppression could be replaced in America, he warned, by "infidelity and atheism" ("The Sons of Italy" 191). Protestants in America had to evangelize the Italians, he implored, "not only for the salvation of the Italians, but for the salvation of America as well" (191). In an era of ever-increasing anti-immigrant sentiment, it was important for di Domenica to say that his fellow Italians could become good Americans.

Protestant ministers and writers sometimes discussed in their writings which Protestant faith might be most appropriate for Italian immigrants. Joel S. Ives, leader of the Congregational Home Mission in Connecticut during the late nineteenth and early twentieth century, said (1905): "The freedom of the Congregational way appeals to the Italian" ("Italian Connecticut" 301). And three years later he stated in words that make a direct connection between religion and Americanization: "If it is good for the Yankee it is good for the Italian.

Experience has proven it good not only for religion, but for citizenship" ("Italy in Connecticut" 609). On the other hand, Lilian Skinner, a church worker with Italian immigrants in Rhode Island, argued that the Episcopal Church would be the best choice for such immigrants "because here in the United States is a Catholic Church, American, not Roman, paying allegiance to no foreign authority, yet a Church authoritative, sacramental [. . .] Moreover our Church, with its noble and dignified service, meets their need of worship in the accustomed way" (101–102).

F. C. Capozzi, the long-serving Italian-born Pennsylvanian Episcopal, conjectured in his late-life essay: "what if the concept of authority on which Rome's assurances are based, should derive from the imperial traditions of the Caesars, rather than from the spirit and teachings of the Nazareth Carpenter?" ("Where I Found God" 15). Capozzi believed this to be the case and this theory formed the thesis of his 1918 study *Protestantism and the Latin Soul*. Capozzi argues for American Episcopalianism here by arguing against both most Protestant faiths and the Roman Catholic Church. He says that Italians are psychologically unfit for Protestantism because most denominations provide too much freedom, and while Italians may be psychologically matched to Catholicism, that Church has been too corrupted and debased over the centuries. According to this interesting theory, "The development of the religious character follows closely that of the characters of tribes and races" (108). Papal Catholicism, he says, "is a religious system closely connected with the tradition and genius of the people who elaborated it" (116), and such "tradition and genius" is "an heritage left her [. . .] by the Roman Empire" and not by the word or acts of Christ (115).

One Baptist minister from the same generation began his conversion in part after being convinced that Protestants did not use sorcery, and when he witnessed a Protestant minister build for himself a fire in a stove—for in Italy a servant would always do such a task for any priest. Francesco Sannella went on to be one of the leading Italian missionary Baptists in America. Coe Hayne (June 1924) in telling Sannella's conversion narrative in *Missions*, noted, "In America opportunities come to boys and girls with stout hearts and high purpose. Francesco had been a saver of money as well as a hard worker" (353): an interesting Ben Franklin–like moral to draw from Rev. Sannella's life story. The Baptist faith, in other words, was right for Sannella and Sannella was right for America.

One of the leading Baptist editors and writers of the early twentieth century claimed that "the northern Italians are of Keltic stock, closely akin to the French and Swiss, and have carried their civilization to a higher development than have the Iberians who inhabit the south of Italy" (Grose, *The Incoming Millions* 59). Grose, nonetheless, believed the Southern Italians coming to the United States could become Americans, and that the Protestants of America must make certain that they do so.

The year before the publication of Grose's 1906 book, Kate Holladay Claghorn wrote a similar opinion in an article titled "Our Italian Immigrants." She, too, pointed to divisions and differences: "A dark picture is often drawn of the incoming hordes of Italians, especially of those from the south" (177). Northern Italians, she said, are "more prosperous, more intelligent, in a higher stage of industrial development than the south" (177), and while those of the south are poor and illiterate (178), she added, "the recent history of this people seems to show that they are not degenerate and degraded, but simply undeveloped; and that they are passing through their present stage as an incident of a journey upward and not downward" (179). Below these words appeared the picture of a group of people on two sides of the image and a young boy in the middle of it, and beneath them are the words: "Raw Italian Material for American Citizenship" (179). Although these Protestant writers incorporated pseudo-scientific racial taxonomies of regional stereotypes in their conceptualization of Southerns, that is, Southerners were less evolved compared to "superior" Northerners, they believed these Southerners had been impeded by environment rather than a fixed biology. As a result, they believed the racial evolution of Southern immigrants could be improved by environmental forces available to them through the Protestant ministry and churches. Through Protestantism, so they believed, immigrants could evolve into true Americans. A few years later Grose (1909) became even more emphatic regarding the centrality of Protestantism in America and for immigrants to America. "The supreme truth to be realized," he said, "is that nothing but Christianity, as incarnated in American Protestantism, can preserve America's free institutions" (*Aliens or Americans* 255).

The Italian Congregational Church of Hartford, Connecticut organized the 1938 Columbus Day celebration for the capital city. The Church's men's club, called the Thomas Hooker Club, had prepared "special exercises." Here we see the Italians both maintaining their (newly discovered) *italianità* and entering the city's dominant cultural life. It is an "Italian" Congregational Church (Congregationalism was once the state religion of Connecticut), and the men's club has been named after the Anglo-Puritan founding father of Connecticut. On this Columbus Day, a civil holiday, Rev. Natale Ricciardi spoke in Italian on "Columbus's Glory and Faith" and Dr. Joseph Paladino spoke in English on "Columbus's Greatness." "America, the Beautiful" and "O, Italia, Beloved" were sung (*The Hartford Courant*, October 12, 1938, 1).

Before his retirement Rev. William Zito served as pastor at the Watertown, Connecticut Congregational Church for thirty-four years. His father came to America as a young man, returned to Italy, married, and returned with his wife to America. They settled in Hartford and had eight children, William being the youngest. One child died in infancy and, as Rev. Zito told me, the local Catholic priest would not conduct the burial service without a payment (Barone, interview with Rev. William Zito). A family friend told the Zito parents of a Congregational minister who preached nearby and in Italian! The Zito's movement away from Catholicism and into Protestantism, therefore, resulted from the obstinacy—as the parents viewed it—of an autocratic and self-indulgent priest.

Rev. Zito told me his family became somewhat ostracized by others in the Italian American Catholic community, but later some of their relatives joined them at the Congregational Church where, Rev. Zito said, there was a true feeling of community, more meaning and less ritual, and Bible study. Zito also told me that while a student at the Hartford Seminary, he would sometimes receive quizzical responses when he told others that he was preparing to be a Congregational minister. William Abbate, on the other hand, told me: "Ostracized, No!" (e-mail correspondence to Barone, June 12–14, 2009). Abbate is the grandson of Rev. Paolo Vasquez of Saint Paul's Italian Episcopal Church in Hartford. Abbate explained that Saint Paul's had a central location in the Italian neighborhood and that many Italians sought his grandfather for his expert fluency in English. In addition, Paolo Vasquez came from a well-known affluent family in Canicattini Bagni in Sicily, and many of Hartford's Italian immigrants also came from Canicattini. Furthermore, Saint Paul's was not a Protestant evangelical storefront mission, but rather a stately edifice with "statues of saints and votive candles that parishioners could use, something not seen in many Episcopal Churches" (e-mail correspondence to Barone, June 12–14, 2009).

Rev. Zito's Congregationalism may be farther from high church architecture and ritual than an Episcopalian one, but the New England plain style may be perceived, and certainly was so perceived in the early twentieth century with its popular Colonial Revival, as the apotheosis of American culture. (The Colonial Revival with its nostalgia for an idealized past can be viewed as a response to challenges of modernism such the global migrations of peoples.) Rev. Zito said that Congregationalism did provide a smooth transition into the American mainstream, but also allowed for a continuing identification as Italian. His children and grandchildren, he said, identify themselves as Italian American. He told me this anecdote: one of his sisters and her best girlfriend were both at the top of their high school class. Rev. Zito's sister obtained employment with an insurance company because she was Protestant, while his sister's friend—an Italian Catholic—found a job at a laundry.

"My grandparents got doors opened by folks associated with their new American friends. Industrialists gave them jobs. Kind hearted folks saw that their children got to summer camps. Many helpful blessings flowed from their associations." Thus, Paul Vizzini reported to me regarding his grandparents who attended Ariel Bellondi's Italian Baptist Church in Lawrence, Massachusetts (e-mail correspondence with Barone, June 4–6, 2009). Because his grandparents attended Bellondi's church and because they befriended English-speaking Americans, Vizzini told me, "they spoke English faster and better than their peers." He added, "I can recall a retired Baptist missionary lady that was a frequent guest at their home, a Miss Bessie Smith. She didn't speak a word of Italian so the conversation was in English."

Bellondi performed Vizzini's grandparents' wedding, "the first among the Italian immigrants at the Baptist church in Lawrence." The minister presented two carnival glass vases filled with flowers, perhaps indicative of all that might bloom from this union in American soil. Vizzini has these vases on his living room mantle today in Phoenix, Arizona, where he has done volunteer work to assist "Hispanics with acclimating to the USA." He told me, "It's just my way of trying to give back to others a little of what was given to my family many years ago. [. . .] I feel that if I have been blessed, I need to be a blessing to someone else" (e-mail correspondence with Barone, June 4–6, 2009).

∽

Historians of immigration have often remarked that emigrants from the newly or recently unified peninsula identified with their town, and with neither region nor nation. The old joke is that Italians did not know they were Italian until they got to New York. I might add that something similar occurred to a lesser extent with Catholicism; their Catholic identity became revivified or re-created in the United States. Over time and across generations Italian Americans forgot the "tyranny" of the Catholic Church and the state's exploitation of the South. Indifference became replaced by a sort of *cultural amnesia*. And so the children of immigrants and the children of the children of immigrants may say they are of Italian heritage rather than Calabrian, and they may also believe that all Italians are Catholic. For a truer and fuller understanding of the Italian American past, it is necessary to remember the persistent option of Protestant conversion and faith.

Rev. Mangano closed the Italian Department of the Colgate-Rochester Divinity School in 1932, for he saw changes occurring: "restricted immigration," and "greatly improved living conditions" ("The Closing of the Italian Department" 4). He added in his remarks: "The novelty of our message has worn off. But in addition to this the omnipresent moving picture theater has militated against our work" (4). Perhaps these Protestant immigrant churches of various denominations, though their numbers were always small, had too much success in making immigrants feel at home in America. In a sermon he delivered after twenty years in Hartford, Rev. Paolo Vasquez of Saint Paul's Italian Episcopal Church, complained that his congregation had become too materialistic (too American?): "We think more of earthly things than about Heavenly matters," he said (*The Hartford Courant* April 22, 1929, 3). Nonetheless, at this time Mangano thought Italian Protestant churches still a necessity in America, even if he had to close his Italian Department (a program founded in 1907, and designed for the training of Italian immigrants as Baptist pastors to minister to the needs of fellow immigrants). Mangano gave three reasons for such churches to continue: "to strengthen family unity," to provide young Italian-Americans with "more personal attention than they are likely to receive in any American church," and because "our Italian churches are located in districts where there are no American churches" (6).

But the Italian churches did fade away. Italian Americans did remain Protestant but joined local nonethnically specialized churches, and Italian Americans are very prominent today as ministers in every

Protestant denomination and in the Episcopal Church. In Hartford, Connecticut, one of the last ministers to attend to needs of a specifically Italian congregation was Natale Ricciardi, who did not retire until 1976. *The Hartford Courant* reported on the occasion of Ricciardi's retirement that he served the Italian community for forty-six years but now there are only "a few old-timers who need his help" (May 1, 1976, 19). The article reported that according to Pastor Ricciardi, "As the Italian population around Hartford became more prosperous and more assimilated, the Italian ministry became less important" (19). The Hartford Italian Congregational Church, which had begun in 1903 under the guidance of Rev. Pasquale De Carlo, merged with South Congregational Church in 1963.

Each October in the United States is National Italian Heritage Month. Though it is a month to commemorate the Italian American past and the contribution of Italians to the United States, one aspect of Italian heritage is all but forgotten. All but forgotten are the Italian American Protestants. They are almost beyond memory because everyone assumes that anyone of Italian identity must be Catholic, but this is not so. They are almost beyond memory because the Italian American Protestant churches are gone, their members having long ago merged with older mainstream churches, and it is therefore difficult to recall this somewhat forgotten past.

But it is not impossible to recall. For example, while driving west on Richmond Hill Avenue in Stamford, Connecticut, look to your left and you'll see the One-Way Church of the Apostolic Faith. One-hundred years ago this simple and plain chapel housed the Italian Baptist Church (one of the churches served by my great-grandfather). Or pause for a moment while entering the modern First Congregational Church on the green in Waterbury, Connecticut, and read the plaque honoring Rev. Pasquale Codella, an Italian immigrant who for decades ministered to the city's immigrants.

We can recall that in 1917 24 percent of the population in Bridgeport, Connecticut was Italian, and this city had the first Italian Congregational church in America to worship in its own building, Calvary Congregational, Rev. Canio Cerreta presiding. In the year 1917 there were nineteen Italian Baptist churches in Connecticut, eleven Congregational, two Episcopal, and two Methodist (Mangano, *Religious Work Among Italians* 43, 46–49). Rev. Paolo Vasquez's stately church edifice on Grove Street in Hartford, Connecticut is long gone, replaced by a corporation's employee parking garage. Some grandchildren of his parishioners remember the church. They might attend a suburban church or have rejoined the Catholic Church or do not practice any faith tradition, which today in the second decade of the twenty-first century may be the most American option of them all.

Like the Southern Question, the Roman Question also influenced and shaped life in Italy and America. What that question asked and meant and how it became manifest in some literary works will be discussed in the subsequent chapter.

Chapter 4

Answers to the Roman Question

Rome is eminently worth saving.

—D. G. Whittinghill, "Baptist Work and Prospects in Italy"

What was the Roman Question, and why did it need to be answered? The establishment of an independent and unified Italy necessitated the victory of nationalistic forces against the military of the Holy See, particularly in the Papal States, a large region in central Italy that included Rome. Nationalistic forces eventually succeeded; in 1870 Rome became the new nation's capital, and the Pope lost his temporal power. As Peter D'Agostino has written, "The Holy Father called upon Catholic states and his faithful children in non-Catholic states to participate in his incessant rituals of protest. Liberal Italy, on the other hand, had the backing of liberals, Protestants, and Jews the world over. It [. . .] contended the pope was a spiritual leader who did not need to rule land in order to carry out his religious mission" (*Rome in America* 1). While American Protestants celebrated these events, American Catholics believed that a tyrannical government had imprisoned Pope Pius IX. In other words, one can say, these events and reactions oftentimes had as much to do with politics as religion. The Protestants praised the birth of a new modern nation, and the Catholics condemned the secularism of that state.

The crucible in which Italian immigrants to America lived had many elements. Catholic immigrants confronted the control of the church by Irish clergy who relegated Italians to church basements, did not speak their language (both literally and figuratively), found many of their practices primitive and pagan, and blamed them for the Pope's defeat. Furthermore, "Although American Catholics universally condemned Liberal Italy, Italian Catholics were divided" (D'Agostino *Rome in America* 42). In addition, Protestant missions offered Italian Catholic immigrants an array of services before and more effectively than Catholic efforts such as those of Bishop Scalabrini and Mother Cabrini. Two other elements in this Italian immigrant cauldron were the Italian liberals who criticized the Church for its antimodernist and antidemocratic views. Last, there were political alternatives such as Anarchism and Socialism that clashed with the mainstream assimilation efforts of Americanization.

Peter D'Agostino, the leading scholar on the Roman Question, has written that overtime "as the Vatican eased its condemnations of the Italian state, this 19th century tension gave way to a pervasive Catholic ethnic nationalism cultivated by priests and laity, in league with the Italian government and non-sectarian organizations such as the Order Sons of Italy in America" ("The Religious Life of Italians" 73). Remnants of these conflicted feelings, however, remained long after. Orsi has written that Pope Leo's "concern for the immigrants provided him with both an opportunity to demonstrate that the Vatican cared about the Italian people and with a chance to embarrass the government in Rome by showing that it cared for them more than the government did" (64). At times, intrigue, manipulation, and calculation characterized actions undertaken from every position, including various Protestant ones. In a comical way, we will see this momentarily in the opening chapter of Josephine Gattuso Hendin's novel *The Right Thing to Do*.

My concern here remains primarily about Protestant actions in what D'Agostino calls the "contest for hegemony over Italian Americans" (*Rome in America* 52). In addition to Hendin's novel, literary examples of various ways of thinking about the Roman Question follow, and these include writings by Elena Gianini Belotti, Antonio Arrighi, Pietro di Donato, and Charles Calitri.

∽

In Josephine Gattuso Hendin's 1988 novel *The Right Thing to Do*, the antagonist Nino Giardello; a conservative, Catholic, college-educated middle-aged, Sicilian-born man living in Queens, follows his college-age American-born daughter, the novel's protagonist, Gina, into Manhattan one day. They pause at Washington Square where they each ponder a statue of Risorgimento leader Giuseppe Garibaldi. They look at the same object, but they see it in different ways. This similarity and difference express their antagonism and their connection. I believe Hendin repeats the phrase "the right thing to do" twenty-two times in the novel, and usually she has Nino proclaim it or worry about it. What is "the right thing to do"? Curiously perhaps, Nino looks at Garibaldi and sees an emblem of masculinity, not a jailer of the Pope or an anti-Catholic Protestant as many American Catholics would have in the not too distant past. The time period for this novel is the 1980s, and the Roman Question has been answered, though perhaps not fully resolved as the book's first chapter demonstrates. For Nino and daughter Gina the conflict embodied by the statue is one of gender and not of faith. For Nino, Garibaldi "was the kind of man you could see would use his sword to defend the right things. [. . .] There was a man for you" (79). This tarnished image, as Gina sees it, furthermore becomes ironic for, as Hendin writes: "What hypocrisy, a petty tyrant like him [Nino] talking about a liberator" (80).

While Garibaldi embodies either human greatness or human limitation and neither Nino nor Gina expound on either political liberalism or anticlericalism, the novel opens with a scene that brings together anticlerical views and differences within the established Catholic Church along ethnic lines. Nino's sister, Maria, has died. The Irish priest who came to deliver last rites leaves without doing so, for Maria had told the priest, as Laura, Nino's wife and Gina's mother, recalls: "'that all religions were the same'" (4).

The priest did not appreciate Maria's ecumenical spirit. Nino says his sister made the statement only because a Protestant was in the room. Laura believes the Irish priest demonstrated his rigidity, cold-heartedness, and obsession with a strict adherence to rules. (Recall that Rev. William Zito, a long-serving Congregational minister in Connecticut, told me his immigrant parents moved away from the Catholic Church and into the Congregational because a Hartford priest would not conduct a burial service for one of their children.) Nino says his mother had been a Protestant back in Sicily, and Laura says, "'Spitting at the Bishop of Palermo instead of kissing his ring doesn't make you a Protestant'" (5). Nino defends his mother saying, "'She did it because the Church never did anything to help . . .'" (5). Meanwhile, they still have Maria, dead, propped up in a chair in her Queens apartment as if she were still alive. They ponder what to do. Nino thinks one must "harden" oneself "to the Church's hypocrisy," and that he must see to it that Maria has a proper burial so that Gina does not get any incorrect notions. Yes, Nino believes he must do the right thing. Nino's nephew, Vinnie, suggests they move his mother to his place on Mulberry Street—the old Italian neighborhood of lower Manhattan—for there the Italian priest, Father Romano, will be more flexible than the Irish one in Astoria, Queens. Nino thinks, "It was even right for Maria to go back to the old neighborhood" (12), and Vinnie says, "'Father Romano is OK'" (13). Laura insists that they tell the young family members, including Gina, that Maria died and nothing more, not that they snuck her corpse out of one building and transported her to another one in an entirely different neighborhood in a different city borough. Laura asks, "'How can you make them respect religion if they know what you have to go through just to make the Church do the right thing?'" (16). To which Vinnie replies, "'Those Irish twerps aren't the Church. Romano with all his faults understands more'" (16). In this example conflict between Irish and Italian Catholics underscores the characters' ambivalence regarding religion in general.

Based in part on a notebook that belonged to her father who suffered terrible immigrant horrors in America and eventually returned to Italy, Elena Gianini Belotti's novel *The Bitter Taste of Strangers' Bread* (*Pane amaro*) offers a brief respite from hunger and humiliation for its main character, Gildo, and his companions. "One dismal day," Belotti writes, "after wandering around aimlessly, tired and numb and not knowing where to go, Gildo, Luigino, and Giusepi sought shelter in a protestant church [sic] [. . .]" (168). This church is warm, whereas the local Catholic Church reminded them "of the glacial temperature of the parish church in Abbazzia [. . .]" (168). In the Protestant church, these men marvel at the fact that they are each served "a smoking bowl of tasty stew [. . .]" (168). How can this be, they wonder? A "Catholic Church wouldn't dream" of serving meals to hungry Protestants (169). Luigino conjectures that the women of this Protestant church "were good Samaritans who didn't care what church they belonged to, but only wanted to lighten the suffering of the emigrants [. . .]" (169). These men, who didn't understand the difference between Catholic and Protestant and did not particularly care, returned frequently for more hot meals and they attended services and tried to sing the English-language hymns. They reason, "in Abbazzia they sang in Latin and didn't understand a bit of that either" (169). Like Maria in *The Right Thing to Do*, these "Catholic" men believe all religions are similar. It would not be an apostasy to convert, "seeing that it was the same Jesus" (169). The men had lost what faith they had before coming to America, and in the drudgery of their work they began to "mistrust" "any religious practice and belief" (170). They take advantage of the Protestant church's goodwill all through an otherwise difficult winter. They hear of work in Oregon, and all of the gang but one decides to go. "Before leaving the city," Belotti narrates, "they said goodbye to and thanked the good people at the Protestant church who had been so kind to them" (173). And that's it. There is no mention of Protestant goodwill again in the novel. Is this moment of calm but an aspect of narrative development? Gildo leaves hopeful that his luck in America has changed. It hasn't. And his life declines unimaginably in the subsequent pages. Since the Protestant mission appears just before midpoint, is its presence in the novel mostly rhetorical?—offer the reader (as well as Gildo) some hope and then descend into scenes that are perhaps crueler than those in any other story of immigrant travail. Nonetheless, for Gildo and his friends, the Protestant church offers a hot meal in a new land while the Catholic Church met their needs with cold indifference.

∽

After the unification of Italy, Rev. Antonio Arrighi yearned for his homeland. "Italy was now open to the preaching of Christ's Gospel," he wrote in his memoir, "and my heart was burning with intense longing to go there as the herald of a free salvation" (231). He sailed for Italy "in the spring of 1871" (232), and he noted his reaction to the newly formed nation as follows:

> Italy was no longer the country of tyranny and slavery. It was not now divided into small States, over which a more

> or less imbecile potentate ruled. Neither was it [any] longer the land of universal illiteracy, but free and united under the liberal dynasty of the House of Savoy. Italian commerce had doubled. The land was no more priest-ridden. The great saying of Mazzini and Cavour had been fully realized, "A free Church in a free State." (232)

At the Methodist Episcopal Church Mission in Bologna he heard the Gospel in his "own sweet tongue" for the first time. He recalled, "The name of Jesus never sounded more precious than it did on that occasion" (233). In the midst of such reverie and narration, he pauses, interrupts his chronology with a parable or folktale about a bridge, a dog, a priest, and the devil. This legend concerns the Ponte del Diavolo (the Devil's Bridge) in the town of Borgo a Mazzano. The story in Arrighi's telling becomes an anticlerical, if not pro-Protestant, one. In it three times images cannot take the place of faith.

The town needs a bridge across the fast-flowing water of a river, but no one can figure out how to construct one here. The priest instructs his parishioners to pray to patron saint San Rocco. The townspeople form a procession with a statue of their beloved saint. Alas, nothing happens: "no response was made to their prayers, no bridge came into being" (236) by carting about a saint's image.

Next the baker suggests that they solicit Satan's aid. Surprisingly, they all approve of the plan, except the priest. Just then a stranger appears and "at his heels the forked end of a tail was visible" (237).

The townsmen are afraid and "they frantically crossed themselves in the hope that the sign of the cross would make the devil flee. Instead it made him laugh in derision" (237). Finally, the third image comes into the Protestant parable: the men turn to the parish priest who takes his crucifix and waves it at "Signor Diabolus" (237). The first moral of the story follows. The devil says,

> "Shame on you, Christians, to confide in the sign of the cross, instead of having real faith in Him who died on it! It is not the cross that frightens me, but the sacrifice made thereon. [. . .] You trust in a mere symbol; yes, you worship an idol, and at the same time you neglect Him whose name you bear. The people I fear are those who have true faith [. . .]." (238)

Nevertheless, the devil agrees to help. He will construct a bridge for the town on one condition, "'and that is this: the first soul to cross the bridge shall be mine!'" (239). All agree to the devil's terms. The priest nominates the baker to be the first to cross the bridge; the baker nominates the priest. The baker curses and the devil chastises all present in a manner that pokes fun at these people and their churches. He says, "'No profane language in my presence! You may swear in your churches, but in the presence of Satan cursing is forbidden'" (239–240).

Next, the devil gets impatient and complains his "'time is short'" and he is "'a busy person'" (240). Nonetheless, he agrees once more to build the bridge, but reminds them again of their bargain.

They wake the next morning and they have their bridge, but no one will dare cross it. Noon approaches and the devil once more becomes impatient. "Just then a yellow dog happened to come near the priest, and instantly he formed his plan" (241). The priest pushes the dog on to the bridge, gives it a firm whack with his cane, and then the dog runs across the bridge away from the priest. Since in this village the townspeople believe that dogs have souls, the priest has tricked the devil. Arrighi delivers another punch-line or moral: "There is an old saying in that part of the country that the cunning of a priest is greater than that of a devil" (243).

Arrighi then returns to his chronological narrative and next recounts his return to his hometown. "There was great rejoicing at" his return by everyone, except the local priest. The priest tries to have Arrighi arrested, but the officer inquires, "'what crime has the young man committed?'" (248). The priest replies, "'he is a renegade from our holy religion, and a rebel against the government of our Holy Father, the Pope'" (249). The official will have none of it. He asks, "'Are you not aware that we now have a united Italy, and that we are no longer under the Papal government? [. . .] in Italy we have religious toleration, and every man is free to hold and express his religious convictions'" (249).

There is rhetorical brilliance in Arrighi's interruption of his narrative proper with the insertion of a seven-and-one-half-page Protestant parable and then a return to his own story wherein he comes home triumphant, but the priest of his town and of his past looks both foolish and intolerant. Arrighi forgives the priest. The police official says, according to Arrighi, "'I was born a Catholic and I hope to die such, but really I see a better Christian spirit in the so-called heretic [Arrighi] than in you priests and Jesuits'" (250). The priest continues to argue that Arrighi should be locked up. The officer concludes that the priest is the one who should be locked up for instead of counseling peace the priest sows "'the seeds of discord [. . .]'" (251). In other words, like the priest in the tale of the devil and the bridge, the priest in the author's hometown exercises great cunning and little piety or faith. Arrighi, the Methodist minister, and the Catholic *questore* become good friends.

∼

In an Italian Baptist Mission report (1907), its author notes that after one of Southern Italy's natural disasters—an eruption of Vesuvius— "bigoted Catholics" blame the damaging event on the presence of Protestant evangelists in Boscoreale and Boscotrecase. A procession commenced and the report's author mocks it, saying how can an image held aloft stop a lava flow? "Our papal friends (?)," the report's author sarcastically writes, "were equally foolish when they carried about in processions wooden images of the Virgin and saint hoping thereby to hinder the flow of hot lava and to stop the earthquakes" that followed the eruption.

∼

American novelist Pietro di Donato, on the other hand, speaks of the wondrous miracles of a holy woman, Mother Cabrini, in his biography titled *Immigrant Saint*. If Arrighi's autobiography, published in the early twentieth century, offers full support of liberal Italy, di Donato's mid-century biography condemns it and instead fully endorses the claims of the Catholic Church's late-nineteenth-century leaders in Italy.

Di Donato says nothing of Americanization efforts or Italian nation-building, but instead offers a defense of Papal authority and legitimacy. He takes, then, the Irish American position regarding the Roman Question: that is, the Pope had been wronged by secular Italy, and his temporal power had to be restored. For example, early on in the biography he asserts that "the clergy, beloved of the common people, were dispossessed of many of the lands, and subjected to other forms of tyranny" (4). We have seen that the Protestants endorsed the position that the clergy tyrannized the common people and these people distrusted the clergy. Pope Pius IX, di Donato proposes: "wanted the church kept intact and would not have it enslaved to either nationalism or liberalism" (4). Such strong language as "enslaved" typified the antiliberal position.

Like Arrighi, di Donato, too, tells anecdotal narratives, such as the following, to paint moral pictures. The novelist recalls an early teaching experience of Francesca Cabrini's. On her first morning she attempts to begin the day with a prayer. But "the children were quick to inform her that Mayor Zanardi was of the liberal party, that he was an enemy of the pastor, Don Serrati, and definitely forbade religious instruction in the public school" (23). One of the mayor's children attends Cabrini's class. The young girl so admires her teacher that her father first reconsiders "his view of religion," and then allows Cabrini "to return him to the faith" (24).

In di Donato's famous novel *Christ in Concrete*, the Catholic clergy are condemned (as are all figures of authority). When Paul, the son of the tragically killed construction worker Geremio, goes to his priest for aid and comfort, young Paul learns of the hypocrisy and gluttony of this particular man of the cloth. What di Donato develops in *Immigrant Saint* does not contradict his earlier writing, for one of the blessings of Mother Cabrini, according to di Donato, was her ability to re-inspire those who chose a religious life. As the author puts it: "Her passion for Christ burned new life into cautiously tired, static, and complacent clerics" (54). Indeed, it seems that far more than her organizational skills, it is her "passion for Christ" that di Donato most admires in his subject.

At the beginning of *Christ in Concrete*, Geremio dies in a horrific construction accident that resulted from an Anglo American overseer's attempt to cut costs and increase profits. Geremio's death occurs not only at the start of Easter weekend, but at the very time he and his family were to take possession of the house they so struggled to purchase. In *Immigrant Saint* di Donato similarly condemns the unconscionable money-grubbing of America:

> The father of a Calabrian family had been blinded by acid in a factory. A Sicilian woman bitten by a rat has died from gangrene and left eight children, who roamed the streets like wild animals while the father worked as a construction laborer. [. . .] In every direction before her [Cabrini's] eyes were His children crushed, twisted, and torn in the giant machine of the New World. (74)

Mother Cabrini and the sisters of her order do all they can to alleviate the suffering of Italian immigrants. In di Donato's narrative, Mother Cabrini urges the daughters of the Missionary Sisters of the Sacred Heart: "'We shall produce the beautiful fruit of Christ's love in America'" (75).

When they celebrate their successes, such as the opening of a hospital, the Sisters and Mother Cabrini keep the occasion completely religious. Unlike opening or anniversary days at Protestant institutions such as the Hartford Italian Congregational Church, there are no civic speeches or patriotic songs. Instead, as for example, at the opening of a hospital in Chicago, "The morning ceremony was purely religious and consisted of the blessing of the house by the archbishop, followed by a long procession of people. There was a Solemn High Mass, with a sermon by the archbishop" (177).

Along infamous Mulberry Bend in New York, according to di Donato, Mother Cabrini's work "became the purifying beacon to the Italian quarter" (74), and many in the neighborhood returned to "their Christian exercises" (75). As many scholars have pointed out, the American Catholic Church during the time of large-scale Italian immigration remained under the control of Irish American clergy (and to a lesser extent German American), who found Italian religious customs baffling, if not pagan. Furthermore, as Robert Orsi has written, "the Irish held the Italians responsible for the 'imprisonment' of the pope by the forces of the Italian revolution" (*Madonna* 117). And so Mother Cabrini's passion that provided both a place for her countrymen to worship and reason to do so was one answer to the Roman Question.

~

Pentecostalism might also be considered to have been an answer to the Roman Question. Jon C. Watt speculates that for Italians at the start of the twentieth century, the Pentecostal movement became one possible "response to Irish hegemony in American Catholicism" (176). Watt supports his intriguing thesis by suggesting that this faith offered its adherents a way to resist unwanted Americanization efforts (181) and it enabled "acceptance of the tenets of Christianity without conflicting with traditional folk beliefs and practices" (179)—those very beliefs and practices that so troubled the Irish Catholic hegemony.

The Philadelphia priest F. Aurelio Palmieri in his 1918 article "Italian Protestantism in the United States," published in *The Catholic World*, concluded "Protestantism among Italians" had been "a *complete failure*" (189), and he argued that the main reason for Protestant evangelization of Italian immigrants had been self-preservation and not a concern for the immigrant's spiritual state. According to the priest "there was danger that the continuous stream of Catholic immigrants would out-weigh in the long run the numerical superiority of Protestantism [. . .]. A motive of self-defense, therefore, lies at the bottom of Protestant proselytism, especially among Italians" (180). Or, as the sociologist Theodore Abel put it as late as 1933: "The real issue, as far as the Protestant churches are concerned, is not so much the alleged inadequacy of the Catholic church as the concern for their own position in American life, which is thought to be threatened by the influence of large masses of Catholics" (8). Furthermore, Palmieri argued that all "Italians either are or have to be Catholics [. . .]" (177); they cannot change something that is innate in each individual. Yet, Protestants, as we have seen, for example, in Gino Speranza's writing, argued that the American nation is innately and unchangeably Protestant. If it did change, so the belief went, then it would no longer be "America," but something else.

Italian Protestant preachers asserted that Italian immigrants are not innately Catholic, that their evangelization had been a great success and not a failure, yet conceded that the "numerical superiority of Protestantism" had indeed become a concern, but for different reasons than proposed by Father Palmieri. As Rev. Angelo di Domenica expressed it: "If we desire to bring the Italians into the realm of true Americanism we must give them the Gospel" ("The Sons of Italy" 191). Not only did the Anglo Protestants and the Italian Protestants believe that America had been and should remain a Protestant nation, but they also believed that Italian immigrants were at most nominally Catholic. Di Domenica emphatically asserted such Catholic parishioner half-heartedness in his 1918 essay:

> The professional men and tradesmen are Catholic in name only. They neither attend church nor believe in the priests. The laboring class is composed mostly of illiterates. Even

among them the percentage of those who attend church is very small. It is generally admitted that not quite 10 per cent of the Italians in America support the Roman Catholic Church by their presence in her services. (190)

Whether Italians were innately or nominally Catholic, and whether Protestants proselytized to defeat Catholicism or to save America became much argued topics in these intersecting circles of religion and politics. Although Palmieri claimed the Protestant efforts failed, others, including some Catholics, disagreed. Father John V. Tolino of Philadelphia, for example, rather hyperbolically wrote in 1939 that "there is a tremendous and terrifying leakage of Italians and Italian-Americans from the [Catholic] Church" (22). And slightly to the north in Canada the Methodist minister F. C. Stephenson claimed: "There is no class of European immigrants among whom missionary work is so successful as among the Italians" (quoted in Mangano *Religious Work* 39). In his 1917 book titled *Sons of Italy*, Mangano outlines the various social services provided by Protestant missions and notes that this proved to be an advantage for their evangelization efforts, because during the early years of mass migration the American Catholic churches were indifferent to the sufferings of Italian immigrants. "What is the Catholic Church doing to meet this situation?" he asks rhetorically. "For a number of years it paid little heed to Italians in America. Consequently the work of Italian evangelization was much easier fifteen years ago [1902] than at the present time" (151). Mangano then notes that the Protestant efforts inspired the Catholics to action, adding: "Indeed the pope considered the apathy of the Italian clergy [in America] of such importance that he not long ago sent a special encyclical letter urging them to stop abuses in Italian parishes and do all in their power to hold the Italian people to the church" (*Sons of Italy* 152).

Did the Protestant efforts fail at everything but inspiring Catholics to action? If Italian Episcopal priest Enrico Sartorio's 1918 figures are correct, "[. . .] about four hundred Italian Protestant churches and missions, having a membership of more than twenty-five thousand Italians" (110), then although that is a small number among the millions of immigrants from the Italian peninsula, it is not an insignificant number, and not a "complete failure," as Palmieri asserted. Mangano, however, has a more propagandistic approach to reporting facts and figures. In *Sons of Italy* he uses 1913 figures from *The Catholic Directory* as follows:

> The greatest question confronting the Catholic Church in America is the defection of the Italian immigrant population. In 1912, the Catholic Church made a comparison of Protestant and Catholic statistics, with the astonishing result of 250 Protestant Italian churches to 150 Catholic Italian churches. (153)

Mangano makes no comment about the relative size of these churches. We have seen that many of the Italian Protestant churches were very small. Furthermore, Mangano makes no comparative comment here regarding immigrant attendance and participation in churches not specifically designated as "Italian." And yet Mangano wrote in *Religious Work Among Italians in America* (also 1917) that "the Italian is somewhat timid when he meets with Americans in the church building who are usually not over cordial to the foreigner," and therefore the Italian congregants should "have a separate building" (27). It seems that at times the Anglo Protestants could be as unwelcoming as Irish Catholics were to Italian immigrants.

Nonetheless the Italian-Protestant minister and his Anglo-Protestant colleague often worked together as the following incident will reveal. The 1910 census noted that the city of New Haven, Connecticut had 30,000 Italian residents or 22 percent of the city's population. In 1911 the Italian Catholic church of New Haven asked for an appropriation of $15,000 from the state for an orphanage and school. Three New Haven Italian Protestant ministers—Baptist, Congregational, and Methodist—went to the official hearing in Hartford regarding this funding. Rev. Angelo di Domenica spoke after Rev. Dr. Joel Ives, a leading figure in the Congregational Church of Connecticut. Both opposed the appropriation. Di Domenica argued for the separation of church and state: "If the State should grant money to one church, or to any organization connected with the church, it would identify itself with that church. Such a step is against the spirit and ideals of the Republic [. . .]" (*Protestant Witness* 56). More specifically, he noted: "If the State should grant this appropriation to a Catholic organization, inestimable harm would be done to the work which is being conducted by the evangelical ministers of the State, as some people would come to the conclusion that [. . .] the Catholics are the favored citizens of this Commonwealth and not the Protestants" (*Protestant Witness* 56). The bill was defeated. But two years later the leaders of the New Haven Catholic institution tried once more. Again, di Domenica went to Hartford to argue against the appropriation but before going this time he met with Frank Bishop, a New Haven attorney who also presided over the New Haven Baptist Union. Di Domenica listened to Frank Bishop, went to Hartford, redoubled his efforts to persuade the committee of six state senators, and once again saw the measure defeated. During his speech he noted, "In New Haven we have over 35,000 Italians. There are two Roman Catholic churches and three Protestant churches" (*Protestant Witness* 59).

Perhaps one reason di Domenica spoke so strongly against such an appropriation had less to do with American Constitutional principles or Protestant self-preservation than with the Italian constitution. Despite the enmity between the liberal Italian government and the Catholic Church, the first article of the Constitution stated that the Catholic Church "è la sola religione dello Stato" ("is the sole religion of the State"), but other religions would be tolerated (perhaps).

~

In the typescript obituary for his father, Melchisedec Barone said that Alfredo "at an early age turned his footsteps toward Religion. At 11 years he was a clerk in a Catholic Monastery [in Foggia]. There, like Martin Luther, he found discrepancies of FAITH, and became a Protestant." But he must have continued his education, and he may have journeyed to England for some of his education and then returned to Italy. He certainly must have been widely read. For example, the Library Company of Philadelphia has six anatomy texts that Alfredo Barone brought with him from Italy to America in 1899.

At the end of the nineteenth century and the beginning of the twentieth century the Church not only condemned Italian nationalism, but all things modern: art and science. For example, in 1864 Pope Pius IX issued the Quanta Cura or Syllabus of Errors, which condemned the separation of church and state, freedom of worship, freedom of the press, and modern civilization in general. In 1907 Pope Pius X in two separate documents issued an absolute condemnation of all things modern. In such an atmosphere of rigidity some like Barone and Capozzi embraced other faiths—Baptist and Episcopal in these two instances. And others attempted to reform the Catholic Church from within, to open it to acceptance of new developments in art, science, and polity. This group often met with rebuke and censor. However, Protestantism "proved," as Mangano put it, "an ally of modernism" (49).

The Italian American educator and novelist Charles Calitri wrote a fictionalized account of one such ex-seminarian, ex-priest who embraced higher learning, his father, Antonio Calitri. Charles Calitri called his novel *Father*, a play on the word meaning either priest or dad. Mangano makes an amusing statement regarding ex-priests in *Religious Work Among Italians in America*:

> Ex-priests who enter as workers in our missionary fields are usually the bitterest denunciators of the Roman Catholic Church and of its priests. I shall never forget an expression used by an ex-priest Protestant missionary in speaking about his antagonism toward the class from which he came, before a public audience: "If I had the hearts of all the priests in my hand, I would throw them to the dogs." It is unnecessary to say that this kind of preaching does not make indifferent Catholics favorable to the Protestant position. (23)

While Antonio Calitri did not become a Protestant missionary after leaving the priesthood, he did remain bitter toward it. Instead of a minister, Charles Calitri's father became an educator, a poet, and a translator. Instead of the Bible, Antonio read Dante each night before bed. His dates are 1875–1954, approximately contemporaneous with Alfredo Barone (1869–1950). Can I discover something of my great-grandfather's experience in Southern Italy and with Catholicism by reading Charles Calitri's attempt to discover his father's experience through the writing of a fictionalized account? Charles Calitri's autobiographical novel somewhat like Hendin's has a funeral near (but not at) its start, and somewhat like Belotti's novel Calitri draws from his father's diaries. Calitri's novel moves back and forth from its present and near-present to his father's past, and it traces the late father's life from childhood up to the point when he departs for America. The son has come to Italy to join in the dedication of a new school in the Southern mountain town of Montefumo, a school that is to be named after his father, Guinio Bruno.

Like Calitri's father Antonio, Guinio became a well-known educator, poet, and translator. Though he left Montefumo in his twenties, Guinio became the town's most revered citizen. The fictional son, most likely just as the actual one, feels he knows his American or Italian American father (the son, too, has become an educator and writer), but not his Italian father, because in Italy his dad had been a priest. "I was the son of a priest and had no right to be born" (356), Calitri writes and this is the conundrum he hopes his trip to Italy will help him to figure out.

Like my great-grandfather, Guino Bruno left Italy in 1899. I can say Alfredo and his family left Calitri in 1899, but I cannot visit this town to try to understand the ancestral past, for it was the hometown of neither Alfredo (Salerno) nor his wife Rosina (Bari) nor my grandfather, Melchisedec (Foggia). And the town has been periodically turned upside-down by earthquakes. For Charles Calitri "there was no explanation" for his father's life as a priest in Southern Italy. Yet he searches "for an answer" (29), and this novel is that answer; one that may be more actual than imagined. To answer my questions regarding Italian ancestry, perhaps I must imagine a fictional past more than recount an actual one.

From his youth through his time in seminary and as a practicing priest, Guinio has many doubts regarding Catholicism. At one point he does not bow to a saint's statue, and a fellow priest wants to know why he does not do so. The reply: "'because I thought it would be an offense against God to go on one's knees before wood'" (91). And on another occasion one of his sisters asks him, "'Does the Madonna mourn for her son even when she stands here, and not only during Passion Week when we take her through the streets in search of him?'" To which Guinio replies, "'It is a statue. [. . .] The mother who mourned has been dead for almost nineteen hundred years'" (240). Later, Guinio and a friend form a plan to bring water to the town via an aqueduct, but their appeal for simple engineering becomes thwarted on every side. As Guinio later tells his supportive Bishop: "'Even my colleagues opposed it. [. . .] The people and the clergy both would prefer to pray for rain and to expect miracles of their Saints'" (413). In short, Guinio questions both the perpetuation of old ways and the reluctance to embrace new ones.

Despite the multitude of details and the many tales told in this novel, "even after" he "had come to know of" his "father's priesthood," the son still "had not understood" (337). "The collar had served its purpose," though, the son and author concludes, for without the priesthood his father would not have been able to develop his intellectual capacity (419). Until the trip to Montefumo to speak at the dedication, the son had never known that his father had a school there for the short time between leaving the priesthood and departing for America. This brief period he had known nothing about, but once he learns of this "space between decision and action, the hiatus between his announcement of his going and his final departure," he regards this bridge as "the most important time of all," for it provides unity: "the two pasts in which I had immersed myself were beginning to become one" (437). Now Calitri has his "direct line which led from here to there, from Montefumo to New York" (442).

I know that the British Baptists transferred management of Southern Italian missions to the American Baptists and that left Robert Walker reassigned to the Northern Italy, and Alfredo Barone either adrift or reassigned to America. (My grandfather claimed the latter was the case, though I have not been able to find any evidence to confirm this transfer.) I know that many Calitrani, including Protestant converts, had left for America. And I know that Alfredo's brother had emigrated. But if I were to say, like Charles Calitri, "from here to there" where would "here" and "there" be? *Here* could be Salerno, Foggia, or Calitri. *There* could be Haverhill, Springfield, Monson, East Hartford, Stamford, Lawrence, New Haven, or Brooklyn. At the end of his Italian American family-saga Charles Calitri postulates: "What we seek through all our lives, I thought, is our own beginning, digging even among the silt flats of the riverbeds for stone implements that will tell us we were there, close to the beginning of time" (442). Outside town, at the Ofanto's edge—shall I dig deep, deep, deeper there?

FIGURE 1. This image accompanied Joel S. Ives's essay, "The Gospel for the Italians." Evangelization among migratory workers, Ives said, "is part of the seed-sowing so needful among this large class of our population" (332). In 1903 some eight-hundred Italian laborers worked on the construction of a dam across the Housatonic River in Kent, Connecticut. The electricity created by this project would be used for the cities of Bridgeport and Stamford. Rev. Ives asked, "what shall a little, quiet New England village do with a gang of a thousand 'Dagos' dropped into their midst, almost doubling their population in a day?" ("Gospel" 332). Rev. Canio Cerreta made weekly visits as did Mr. Vincenzo Esperti, colporteur for the Connecticut Bible Society. Ives noted of this photograph: "The exceedingly suggestive picture shows Mr. Esperti preaching from the steps of one of the shanties, and the earnest, attentive faces of the listeners" (332). ("Gospel Service for the Italians," *Home Missionary* 77.9 [December 1903]: 333. Courtesy of the Connecticut Conference United Church of Christ Archives, Hartford, Connecticut.)

FIGURE 2. Bridgeport, Connecticut Calvary Italian Congregational Church, c. 1907. The first Italian Congregational Church in the United States to have its own building. The small sign in front indicates that the church offered language classes in English or Italian every Monday and Wednesday evening. (United Church of Christ Archives, Hartford, Connecticut.)

Figure 3. The Chiesa Apostolica Battista, Monson, Massachusetts. An almost identical image appeared in the October 1901 issue of the *Baptist Home Mission Monthly*, page 287 ("Massachusetts–Monson"). Rev. Barone appears slightly to the left of center in each picture. ("Italian Mission at Monson, Mass." *Baptist Home Mission Monthly* 27:4 [April 1905]: 141).

FIGURE 4. Italian Baptist Church, Monson, Massachusetts. Notice the change from Italian to English in the name of the church. Like the sign in front of the Bridgeport Italian Congregational Church for language classes, this change demonstrates the position of these churches in two worlds. Rev. Barone is on the left. (*Dorcas Society Cookbook.* Monson, MA: Congregational Church, 1906. Courtesy of the Monson Historical Society.)

FIGURE 5. Italian Baptist Church, Stamford, Connecticut. Rev. Vincenzo di Domenica is at the far left and Rev. Barone stands next to him. My grandfather as well as great-aunts and great-uncles also appear in this image, c. 1909. (Courtesy of Fred Verderosa.)

FIGURE 6. Rev. Antonio Mangano. Mangano (1869–1951) and Barone (1869–1950) were contemporaries, though the former had far greater renown in Baptist circles. While Barone did some work in the Springfield, Massachusetts mission early in the century, it was Mangano who joined his former student, Rolando Giuffrida, at the 1928 opening of the Italian Baptist Church of Springfield. More than three-hundred attended that day, including Rev. Francesco Sannella (Barone's former student) (*Springfield Republican* April 30, 1928, 4).

Figure 7. Rev. Dr. Arthur Caliandro "[H]e acted as shepherd, chief encourager, and community builder to a very diverse congregation [. . .]" ("Legacy" 1). Caliandro believed that "There is a place for everyone at God's table. We are all invited, we can all sit down" (*Lost and Found* 227). When preaching Rev. Caliandro wore the robes of a Methodist-Reformed minister. The kindhearted wisdom that this image communicates is the quintessential Caliandro. (Courtesy of Marble Collegiate Church.)

Chapter 5

By Twos and by Threes

I never met my great-grandfather, the Rev. Dr. Alfredo Barone, who was born in Oliveto-Citra-Dogana, Salerno, on May 25, 1869, resided in Calitri from 1892 to 1899, and died in Brooklyn in 1950. While my grandfather Melchisedic and a sister Blandina were born in Foggia, a sister Lydia was born during the years the family lived in Calitri (a fourth Italian-born child died soon after birth). Nine more brothers and sisters were born in the United States. Even though I never met Rev. Alfredo, one family legend that I recall hearing when young—no doubt told to me by my father Alfred—had significant influence; that is, the Rev. Barone had been persecuted and even imprisoned for his beliefs and practices. Not too long ago, I had this legend confirmed for me as historical fact.

In the 1950s, Nunzio Palminota wrote (in Italian), some "Historical Notes about the Baptists in Italy" ("Appunti storici sui Battisti in Italia") that were published in *Il Testimonio*, the long-running publication of Baptists in Italy. In the essay on Calitri, Alfredo Barone and Michele Creanza are the dominant figures. Palminota cites contemporary sources; the article does not rely on reminisces. In it he notes that in March of 1894, Barone—"l'evangelista di Calitri" ("the evangelist of Calitri")—after preaching in nearby Trevico, was arrested and spent nine days in jail.

The late nineteenth century was a time of all sorts of flux, exploration, and unrest in the newly formed nation. What is so fascinating about Calitri is that it seems to have been a very fervent center for spiritual awakening and questioning. The intensity of this small town must be unique. In nearby Trevico, the evangelists would be rejected and persecuted, while in Calitri they would be tolerated by some and accepted by a few. (I have read that there is a Protestant monument with Biblical quotations on it in the town cemetery. Indeed there is a tarnished monument in the section reserved for non-Catholics. All of the inscriptions have worn away except for one word: *Gesù* [Galgano, e-mail correspondence with Barone, November 30, 2014]. Furthermore, Mariagrazia Sheffield—daughter of Italian Baptist pastor Benito Marzano—has told me [October 4, 2014] that carved in stone on top of the door to a house in the oldest part of Calitri, il Castello, are the words, "chi entra qui non trova pace" ["those who enter here do not find peace"]. This house may have been the site of the first meeting of evangelicals in the town.) To say the South or the North, then, has limitations. This shorthand so often used for Italy denies the complexity of experience. In any region—the South, let's say, there is variation and diversity, everything is not only and always one thing. In addition to my great-grandfather, there were three other Italian Protestant pastors in Connecticut who immigrated from Calitri: Rev. Pasquale Codella of Waterbury (Italian Congregational); Rev. Canio Cerreta of Bridgeport (Italian Baptist and Italian Congregational); and Rev. Pasquale De Carlo of Stamford (Italian Baptist), later of Hartford (Italian Congregational), and still later of Chicago (Italian Presbyterian). Rev. Barone's protégé, Francesco Sannella, came from nearby San Sossio. Additionally, I learned that birth records from Calitri for the 1890s listed some children with Biblical names such as Noe Quaranta, Ester Cicoira, Rebecca Cicoira, the Iannolillo brothers: Mose Vincenzo (1892), Iafet Lorenzo (1895), and Sem Luigi (1897). Since my great-grandfather gave eleven of his thirteen children Biblical names, he probably had some influence on this unusual 1890s naming practice in Calitri.

It appears that Alfredo Barone, if not a founder, acted as the guiding force for the Calitri Baptist Church in its earliest years. The English missionary Robert Walker recalled that "our young brother" Alfredo Barone led the church when he (Walker) visited in 1892 ("Calitri"). Walker noted that Alfredo had started a Sunday school (always one of the first initiatives of any Protestant evangelist) and that Rev. Barone ministered to towns across the surrounding region. As already noted, he dedicated his 1895 book *La vita di Gesù Cristo ossia l'armonia degli evangeli* to Walker, "*mio caro sopraintendente*." Baldassare Labanca in his study *Gesù Cristo nella letteratura contemporanea, straniera e itali-*

ana (*Jesus Christ in Contemporary Literature, Foreign and Italian*), said that "Barone has managed to compose more a mosaic of Bible verses than a harmony of the Gospels" ("Il Barone è riuscito a comporre più un mosaico di versetti biblici, che un'armonia degli evangeli") (176). Nunzio Palminota does not elaborate in his brief essay but merely states: "perche se l'Evangelista Barone fu l'iniziatore della chiesa di Calitri nel 1892, il Creanza ne fu il vero fondatore [. . .]" ("For if Barone started the Calitri church in 1892, Creanza was the true founder of it [. . .]") (454). In 1899, Alfredo and family set sail for America aboard the SS *Massillia* out of Naples. Creanza followed as pastor to the Calitri church where he remained until his death in April of 1912.

After arriving in New York, Rev. Barone, his wife Rosina, and their children moved in rapid succession to Haverhill then Springfield and next Monson in Massachusetts. They stayed in Monson for a few years (though Alfredo still traveled from town to town to preach—just as he had in Italy). By 1909, he again became connected with Calitrani when he led the Italian Baptist Church in Stamford, Connecticut (1909–1911). The church, located in an Italian neighborhood on Richmond Hill Avenue, probably had several Calitrani families as congregants. One of the members, Aniello Preziosi, had immigrated from Calitri in 1895 and became a physician in 1910. Unfortunately, he died the same year. Rev. Barone was asked to cocelebrate the memorial service ("Dr. Aniello Preziosi"). I have a photograph that shows Rev. Barone, family and church members, as well as Rev. Vincenzo (Vincent) di Domenica outside this small church building that still stands and still serves an evangelical congregation (the One-Way Church of the Apostolic Faith, Bishop John H. Green). I have copies of some postcards from these years that show two important facts: Rev. Barone had contact with all the major Italian Protestant ministers and he maintained correspondence with residents in Calitri for many years. For example, Alfredo Barone and Donato Cerrata, a leading member of the Calitri Baptist Church, wrote one another for decades.

According to Rev. George Braxton Taylor of the Southern Baptist Convention, ten members of the Calitri church led by Rev. Barone went to Bridgeport, Connecticut, where they attended the Italian Congregational Church (*Southern Baptists* 240). (Italian Protestants were somewhat fluid in their affiliations, and so a Baptist pastor or congregant could easily switch to Congregationalism in another town or vice versa. *The Hartford Courant*, for example, reported in 1903 that Rev. De

Carlo had to explain himself before beginning his work with the Hartford Congregational Italian mission, since he had previously served a Baptist church ["Pastor Installed"]). Whether in America or Italy, the size of congregations was quite small. In 1894 there were thirty-eight adult members of the Calitri Church located on the Via Concezione, entrance on the Vico Stanco. Nonetheless, despite the small numbers the evangelists often expressed exuberant optimism.

Yet, as we have seen, congregants as well as their pastor faced persecution. One year (1907) the Italian Baptist Mission Report noted that at Calitri "a poor widow of this congregation barely escaped a heavy fine and imprisonment because her young son, for whom she must answer, refused to remove his hat while a religious procession was passing in which the usual images were carried. A liberal-minded lawyer freely defended the widow and saved her from a shamefully unjust condemnation. Such is the spirit we must combat in some parts of Italy!" Another yearly report noted that the "Calitri Church is composed of some splendid people. The brethren have been greatly offended by the town authorities, who have put some women of ill-fame near our church in order to disturb our services and bring us into disrepute. Behold another obstacle the devil has put in our way in Italy. He is always assisted in such persecutions by his faithful allies, the priests of the Roman Catholic Church" (1909). And yet another yearly report noted, "In all the country around, Calitri is famous for observance of the Day of Rest" (1900). Rev. Barone played a role in the creation of that fame. When he came to the United States in 1899, he gave as his last place of residence the town of Calitri in the province of Avellino. Barone was not a native of this Irpinian mountain town but he left an imprint of a spiritual nature during his domicile there of about seven years.

The recent DVD produced by the Italian Baptist Church, *Like the Salt of the Earth* (Bemportato and Davite) makes no explicit reference to anything south of Rome and Giorgio Spini's study of the Risorgimento and Protestants, a four-hundred-page book published in 1989, devotes about seven pages to the South (Section Ten, Birth of Italian Evangelism, Part Five, Sicily and the South, pages 315–322—*Risorgimento e protestanti*, "La Sicilia e il Mezzogiorno"). The American Baptists who evangelized in Italy—all across the peninsula—always divided yearly Mission Reports into North and South. I mention this because it seems that there was quite an awakening, an evangelization in the town of Calitri during 1890s, and this story has not been told. Perhaps this successful evangelization remains little heralded, except to those in Calitri today who still carry on this faith, because this mission work came under the auspices of the British Baptists who transferred control to the Americans at the close of the nineteenth century and because, at this time, many residents of Calitri, including those who converted, left for America.

In an e-mail message to me from January 2012, Mariagrazia Sheffield told me that her great-grandfather, Donato Cerreta, "was a very active member in the church in Calitri" and he told Mariagrazia's mother "that the first pastor of the church was Mr. Barone." "Unfortunately," Mariagrazia added, "all the [church] documents that my great-grandfather had kept and were maintained in my grandmother's home were lost in the earthquake of 1980."

But during the 1890s Rev. Walker wrote annual reports for the Baptist Missionary Society of London regarding the work of Baptists in the South, and these reports do survive. Walker, as noted, served thirteen years in Naples as minister for the English Baptist Mission. The Baptist Missionary Society of London began its evangelization in Southern Italy in 1871, and the American Southern Baptist Convention began their work soon after. My great-grandfather affiliated with the former. There is no mention of Barone in Walker's report of 1892 (for the year 1891), and this is interesting. For Walker says that "at present I have two colporteurs laboring in and around one of these towns [. . .] where I hope to see a Mission established ere long" (91). Perhaps the town alluded to by Walker was Calitri, and perhaps Barone was one of the hard-working colporteurs, distributors of Bibles and devotional works. The next year Walker noted that "a very interesting work has been opened up at Calitri [. . .] A colporteur-evangelist, Signor Barone, has been able to initiate a most hopeful movement" (91). Walker also noted that Barone went to many surrounding towns to evangelize and also spoke to "workmen laboring on the new railway [. . .]." "Calitri," observed Walker: "is not the most important of a number of towns in that part of the province, and without special indication would not have been chosen as the centre of a work for the district. But as we had the call to go there, and as God has so evidently blessed the work, it is clear that we must for some time at least look on it as the headquarters of the work we hope to do among these towns and villages" (91). Complimenting Barone, Walker concluded, "I wish it to be distinctly understood that Sig. Barone is a *colpoteur*-evangelist—the kind of evangelist that is really best suited for work of that sort [. . .]" (91).

In his report of 1893, Walker described a visit to Calitri and praised "the order and solemnity of the services," and rejoiced "to see these people intent on reading the Word of God, and to remember that but a few months ago they never thought of it, was very comforting" (91). In addition to the established church's indifference to parishioners' needs and the sense that Protestant faiths might meet personal needs; in addition to the Protestant willingness to embrace modernist thought rather than the outright rejection of all things modern, the attraction of literacy and education more broadly must have been a magnet for the Protestant cause. Reading had a central focus not only to the conversion of those who would become Protestant ministers, but also to the endeavors that these preachers would pursue both in Italy and with Italian immigrants in America. As early as 1874, the English Baptist Edward Clarke reported:

> Literacy and ignorance are the most urgent problems. In a population of twenty-five million Italians only four [million] are able to read and write. I am convinced that the goal of our mission must be together with evangelization a strenuous effort to instruct these people whose rulers for centuries have deliberately left them in ignorance and superstition. (qtd. in Bemportato and Davite)

Whereas Catholicism focuses on the repetition of ritualistic sacraments, Protestantism emphasizes Biblical exegesis. Whereas Catholicism restricted Bible study and offered the priest as sole interpreter, Protestantism distributed Bibles widely and encouraged Bible reading, study, and interpretation by each person. The American writer William Dean Howells included in the first edition of his travel book *Italian Journeys* (1867) a chapter titled "The Protestant Ragged Schools at Naples," in which he wrote that these Protestant schools

> announced that the children would be taught certain branches of learning, and that the whole Bible would be placed in their hands, to be studied and understood. In spite of this declaration of the Protestant character of the schools, the parents of the children were so anxious to secure them

the benefits of education that they willingly ran the risk of their becoming heretics. They were principally people of the lower classes—laborers, hackman, fisherman, domestics, and very small shopkeepers [. . .]. (137)

For his 1894 report on Calitri Walker said that

> This mission continues to prosper, and the little church is continually receiving new additions. Signor Barone has lived down the opposition he met at first, and is everywhere treated by the Calitrani with respect. With the donkey I was able to get for him through the kindness of a friend, he visits several places in the neighbourhood regularly, and in one or two of them has been able to form little groups of Bible-readers. He also gets into contact with the workmen on the new railway, and has evidently won the esteem and respect of the overseers. (90)

And the next year Walker said that Barone continued his good work, particularly among women and workers notwithstanding the continued opposition of Catholic priests. Walker wrote: "In one of his last letters Signor Barone said he felt thankful to the priests, for it seemed as if their opposition sent the people to his meetings" and Walker added, "the feeling of respect for Signor Barone and his work is widening and deepening among the people" (95).

The evangelist encountered various privations as well as jubilation. Barone, as we have seen, faced persecution such as stoning and imprisonment. In the South and all across the peninsula, an evangelist's challenges to the status quo could be called by the Catholic Church explicitly political and therefore in contradiction to Article 1 of the Constitution, which could then result in censoring or imprisonment of an evangelist. For example, according to George Braxton Taylor, Ercole Volpi, a Baptist evangelist in Bari, "was arrested, put in irons, and imprisoned as a Socialist; it was a case of persecution for the gospel [. . .]" (*Southern Baptists* 150).

As reported in *Il Testimonio* (April 1894), Barone spent nine days in jail when the mayor of Trevico claimed that Barone's evangelical activities and discourses were explicitly political and, as such, violated the law and challenged civil order. A lawyer named Antonio

Nicoletti secured Barone's release and exoneration. "Questo processo fu un vero trionfo per l'avvocato, per il Barone e, più di tutto, per la causa dell'Evangelo che ora in questi paesi continua ad esser predicato" ("This process was a true triumph for the lawyer, for Barone, and for the cause of the Gospel that now can continue to be preached in this region") ("Corriere Delle Nostre Missioni").

According to historian Nunzio Palminota's mid-twentieth-century article on the history of evangelization in Calitri, one year prior to Barone's imprisonment, there was "an episode among many: in February 1893 a little girl whose parents were evangelical died, and the priests stepped forward to drive the crowds to believe that Protestants would be buried like animals in a filthy place." ("Un episodio fra tanti: nel febbraio 1893 avvenne la morte di una bimba di genitori evangelici, e i preti si diedero dattorno per far credere al popolo che i protestanti sarebbero stati seppelliti come tante bestie in un luogo immondo" [454]). These examples could be supplemented with hundreds of others. Some in the Catholic Church resorted to acts of slander, intimidation, and violence in an attempt to suppress Protestantism.

The evangelists faced other challenges. As Rev. Walker stated in his 1898 report: "Want of work and sickness have made life very difficult for many of our people, and in this respect things do not seem to improve. The heavy taxes which the Government imposes on almost everything make it increasingly difficult for working people to live, and drive large numbers out of the country altogether" (117). And so in Calitri the completion of the railroad took away some believers and possible converts, and the promise of America took away many others. In the words of Walker: "Some of the best converts are in America, driven from home by the difficulty of getting a living" (117–118).

Another significant change occurred in 1898, when the English Baptist Mission transferred control of evangelization efforts in the south to the American Baptists under the guidance of Rev. George Boardman Taylor. Barone's mentor, Robert Walker, after thirteen years in Naples, went north and the following year reported from Susa and Meana (Province of Turin). In the 1900 English Baptist report, neither the South nor Rev. Barone are mentioned. Barone in 1899 had left with his young family for America. There are three reasons why he did so: many Calitrani had already gone to the United States, support for the mission had stopped or changed hands, and Alfredo Barone's brother, Giovanni, had emigrated the year before. (For a dozen years in the early twentieth century Giovanni served a Baptist mission in Waterbury, Connecticut.)

These changes demonstrate the established structure of power, the extreme poverty in southern Italy, and the failure of liberal thought to fulfill the promise of the Risorgimento. Religious toleration (never mind freedom) had not been realized, and the poor invariably remained poor. The papal forces may have been defeated, but the Catholic Church maintained much of its power, especially through alliances with large landowners. To adapt a phrase from Giuseppe Tomasi di Lampedusa, something must change so that everything can remain the same. These changes also demonstrate the relation between local, national, and global politics: events in cosmopolitan London had an impact in far away provincial Calitri.

∼

Late in the fall of 2009 the town of Monson's Conservation Commission in conjunction with the Opacum Land Trust entered into partnership to purchase 165 acres, known as the Flynt Quarry Land. This land could have become a subdivision of 100 to 125 homes (Opacum Land Trust)—its history completely lost. The Flynt Quarry was the largest and longest lasting of several quarries in the area. It opened under the auspices of the US government at the turn of the eighteenth to the nineteenth century, became the W. N. Flynt Granite Company in 1839, and continued until the 1930s. Stone from the Flynt Granite Company can be found in New York City's Saint Francis Xavier Church, in Connecticut's Nathan Hale Monument, and in a number of remarkable buildings in the town of Monson itself. In the year 1900, 3,403 people lived in the town; in 1905, 4,343; and in 1960, 2,100 (*History of Monson*). At the start of the twentieth century, immigrants formed Monson's swelled population and among these recent immigrants were three-hundred Italian quarry workers.

After one trip to Monson and finding very few Italians listed in town directories, I asked the town historian how she accounts for this. She told me the immigrant quarry workers can be found in other documents (town reports) but only listed as "Tonys" or as numbers—that is, Italian worker one, Italian worker two, and so on (Swierad e-mail correspondence with Barone, March 25, 2010). On that trip I also went to the Palmer Library to look at microfilm. A check of first page headlines and the Monson News section of the Palmer, Massachusetts *Journal Register* for the years 1901–1904 provided one front-page article on the Italian Baptist Church of Monson, a few Monson News mentions of Italians who had been accused of committing one petty crime or another, and none on immigrants or manufactories. News on mainstream Protestant religious speakers and basketball scores seemed of much importance during those years.

According to the *New York Times* in 1891, there was a forty-five-day strike at Flynt Quarry ("Telegraphic Brevities"). Two years later, the *Hartford Courant* reported a violent fight between Irish and Italian workers. One man stabbed another in the throat and another got struck in the head by an ax ("Fight in Monson Quarries"). What was the relation between these events; was there any, I wondered?

A decade later Rev. William Harrison Eaton, Secretary of the Massachusetts Baptist Missionary Society—the oldest organized Baptist body in America—noted in his *Historical Sketch*, a sketch of over four hundred pages, that the "overwhelming tide of immigration" has made Massachusetts "more foreign than any other State in the Union" and this situation, he said, creates both demands and opportunities (124). By the latter, he meant opportunities for evangelization.

Rev. Eaton visited Monson in 1901 and reported in the *Baptist Home Mission Monthly* that "the wretched surroundings, the unsanitary conditions, the squalor, the swarms of children, appeal to me with overwhelming force" ("Massachusetts–Monson" 287). Deacon Domenico Piscitelli led efforts in Monson to organize a small number of Baptist converts, most of whom had been converted before coming to America. They built a chapel on top of one worker's house and petitioned for a permanent preacher. The converted wrote to Baptist authorities: "Rev. A. Barone is here with us for a few days, we have known him for years, he having preached to us before in Italy, we all love him, and as we know that he is experienced in this work, we in the name of God request you to let us have him here to guide the new church" ("Massachusetts–Monson" 286–287).

Five years later, *Home Mission* editor Howard B. Grose in his book *Aliens or Americans?* offered the Monson Italian Baptist Church as an inspiring example. "In devotion and liberality," Grose noted regarding this mission church, "the converted aliens often set noble examples for American Christians" (284). At first, Grose states, the Italians "had no meeting-place, and in this emergency one of the converts proposed that a room be built on the roof of his cottage. This was done by the little band," Grose continues, "and there they worshiped until the place was too small." He concludes, "This indicates the ingenuity as well as the generous and self-sacrificing spirit of these Italian Christians, who maintain a regular pastor and full services" (283–284).

Various improvements were made during Rev. Barone's brief tenure. He oversaw the improvement of the church building and added sewing and evening schools ("Does This Appeal to You?"). One of the first things one can note looking at surviving photographs of the church structures is that the Chiesa Apostolica Battista (1901 photo) became the Italian Baptist Church (1906 photo). This name change may be the first sign of decline—a shift from Italian to English that renders the need for a separate church unnecessary. In addition to a change in dominant language, residential patterns, and class mobility often signal the demise of a church devoted to the evangelization of immigrants. As the Italian American Episcopal priest Enrico Sartorio noted, "Those to reap the benefit of [the Italian evangelical pastor's] work will be the American churches, into whose fold the element prepared by the Italian work will enter" (112).

At Monson, Barone oversaw the official recognition in October 1904 of the church by the Westfield Baptist Association and the congregation grew from seventeen to thirty-eight members and twenty-five Sunday school students ("Italian Baptist Church" 1). Yet, always there was the threat of less quarry work. The 1905 Westfield Minutes report: "If the situation does not improve some families will go elsewhere after work. The small amount of work done at the quarries accounts for the small number of new members" (23). Unlike an urban mission whose dispersed members might readily be supplemented by new arrivals, the Monson Italian Baptist Church served too small a population engaged in a single almost preindustrial occupation.

Another problem for the Italian Baptists at the quarry was local Catholics, who in 1906 constructed the Madonna Chapel at the quarry to serve the Italian workers (Plasse). The Westfield Baptist Association Minutes for that year reported:

> This year the Catholic church has planted a mission, where, in connection with the Baptism of an infant, an Italian opened his house to celebrate the event with more of the spirituous than spiritual. The difference between this and the

Protestant element is thus brought into sharp contrast. But in the grace of God the Italian priest has gone away from Monson, because the Italians do not come to his mission, and the Irish priest is left in charge. The gospel light has turned away the Catholic darkness. (23)

Many American Protestants believed there were a civil as well as a spiritual importance in turning away "the Catholic darkness." As Rev. Grose proclaimed in *Aliens or Americans?*, "The supreme truth to be realized is that nothing but Christianity, as incarnated in American Protestantism, can preserve America's free institutions" (255). And so when Rev. Francesco Sannella, Barone's protégé, succeeded Barone after he left for first the Lawrence, Massachusetts, and then the Stamford, Connecticut, Italian Baptist Church, Sannella added "an evening school for the study of Civil Government, so that our members may become good citizens" (Westfield Minutes, September, 1909, 28).

When the following year Gaetano Lisi succeeded Sannella, who also moved on to serve larger urban congregations, the former added an Italian school "teaching the Italian language to our Italian children" (Westfield Minutes, September, 1910, 25). This also had the benefit for the church of attracting students to the Sunday school. Clearly, though, Deacon Piscitelli's devotional dream had begun to change. For a few years after 1911, visiting pastors came from Springfield until services ceased, the church disbanded, and new owners turned the church building into a dwelling house (*History of Monson* 18). Some remaining members of the Italian Baptist Church joined the Monson Congregational Church. In 1931 the Madonna Chapel became a wing-addition to St. Monica's Catholic Mission in nearby Wales (Plasse), and in September 2008 services ended at St. Monica's (Tanguay 1) and this 1,921-square-foot special purpose building, as a real estate ad described it, could be yours for an undisclosed price.

In 1925 Rev. Barone purchased a plot in Woodland Cemetery, Stamford, and a monument from Joseph Cuva Monumental Works. The Barre, Vermont granite block was to be inscribed in "sunk letters [with] the name Rev. Dr. Alfred Barone, Indipendente Ministro" ("Contract for Alfred Barone"). According to this contract the "o" in Alfredo has been dropped but some words in Italian have been retained for identification of occupation. However, when Rev. Barone died in 1950, predeceasing his wife Rosina (Rosa) by six years, the massive stone had but one word inscribed on in: BARONE, accompanied with an Italian royal crest above and a blank book balanced above that crest. Within the crest are the initials *A* and *O* for Alpha and Omega Assembly, the name of the religious society formed by Barone in 1910.

In a special section of the May 1905 *Baptist Home Mission Monthly* titled "The Italians in America," Rev. Samuel H. Lee claimed in opposition to the beliefs of many contemporaries that "In general the Italian is excellent material for American citizenship" but, he later added, "he needs constant inspiring influences" from "an educated minister" (183-184). Even if by twos and by threes, the Rev. Dr. Alfredo Barone must have been such an educated and inspiring influence as Lee had in mind. (The Protestant evangelists were sometimes university-educated men and widely read. The six anatomy texts that Rev. Barone brought with him from Italy to America in 1899, and that are now at the Library Company of Philadelphia, range from Jean Louis Baudelocque's 1810 *Dell' arte ostetricia* to Alexandre Laboulbene's 1883 *Nuovi elementi di anatomia patologica descrittiva ed istologica*.) Not only did Barone mentor the Rev. Sannella, a boy who at first and second meeting threw stones at the Protestant preacher-man, but at Altamura, Italy, province of Bari, according to Rev. George Braxton Taylor, "Many of our brethren from this town have been to America and speak of Monson, Mass., as if it were all one word, and around the corner" (254). Taylor also noted in *Southern Baptists in Sunny Italy* that "The brother [Alfredo Barone] who originated the work at Calitri is now minster at Monson Quarry, Massachusetts, where there are seven brethren who emigrated from the Gravina church" (240). Whether in an American town or an even smaller Italian village there "in the midst of them" (Matthew 18:20), they would find him. Underneath the picture of the Italian Baptist Church included in the *Dorcas Society Cookbook* of 1906, the women of the Monson Congregational Church wrote: "This church owes its birth and prosperity to Rev. Alfred Barronne [*sic*], through his untiring efforts and love for his people the little chapel at the quarry was made possible."

Italian immigrants who became Protestant did not use their new faith as a means to find meaning in suffering but rather for acceptance and welcome in a new environment. Protestantism became for some a means to negotiate old world and new world ways more than it resulted in the alienation of rejection by established American Catholics and Catholic immigrants and condescension by Anglo-Protestants.

As noted earlier in this chapter, one of the first things one can note looking at surviving photographs of the church structures in Monson is that the Chiesa Apostolica Battista became the Italian Baptist Church. These photographs do indeed illustrate some rapid change and yet, I would contend, ministry in contexts of cultural transition can have enduring impact even if that ministry is impermanent. After Monson, Rev. Barone moved on to Lawrence, Massachusetts; Stamford, Norwalk, and New Haven, Connecticut; and Brooklyn, New York.

From this look at one minister and two churches, *Beyond Memory* next recalls one church in one city: the Italian Congregational Church of Hartford, Connecticut.

Chapter 6

Christ for Hartford

Connecticut was Jordan and the clear
Streams flowing to it marked the Promised Land.

—Wilbert Snow, "Connecticut Tercentenary Ode"

In the early twentieth century, British Baptists in Turin published an English language periodical titled *Christ for Italy: A Quarterly Record of Christian Work and Warfare*. When I came across a reference to this title I considered something: to locate and read it for it must reveal, I conjectured, English attitudes regarding Italian Protestants. To my chagrin I could not locate the quarterly at UK libraries specializing in Baptist materials. I did locate some issues at the Biblioteca Nazionale Centrale di Frienze. Only 1917 and one issue for 1916 seemed to be available and these, the only copies available in Italy. But wait—many such periodicals were damaged in the 1966 flood and moved off-site and still wait, if their condition permits, return to the main library. These difficulties reminded me of my difficulty tracking down a copy of *La vita di Gesù Cristo ossia l'armonia degli evangeli* by my great-grandfather Rev. Alfredo Barone.

And so I moved on to something closer to home, something that would still allow me to consider attitude, in this instance, rather than belief or practice. I read dozens of articles from the *Hartford Courant* (America's oldest continuously published newspaper, founded in 1764) regarding the Italian Congregational Church of this city. What is the image of Italians and more specifically Italian Protestants in this reportage? I also wanted to place this one particular church in the faith environment of Connecticut's capital city. I believed Congregationalism would be ideal for my study because historically it is the church of authority and power in Connecticut, until 1818 the official state religion, and many of the leaders of the Connecticut church in the time of mass-migration were involved in mission work and state politics. I wondered, too, if the Hartford Italian Congregational Church taught elite Asylum Hill Congregational Church anything and would that teaching be revealed between the lines or quite explicitly in the journalistic reportage and related material. By using some church records in conjunction with the newspaper accounts one can establish an interpretation of the attitudes toward an Italian Protestant congregation both from within the group and within the larger surrounding community.

There seems to have been some but not much ecumenical cooperation between the Italian ethnic churches in early-twentieth-century Hartford. When Italia Garibaldi came to Hartford's South Park Methodist Church to present an illustrated lecture on the life of her grandfather, famed Italian nationalist leader Giuseppe Garibaldi, Rev. Vodola (Congregational) and Rev. Roca (Baptist) also sat on the platform (*Courant* September 12, 1910, 13). William Abbate told me, "My grandfather Rev. Vasquez did not consider himself a Protestant. We were Anglican Catholics" and not Protestant Episcopal. He recalled that other Episcopal congregations and the Episcopal hierarchy were very supportive and Saint Paul's Italian Episcopal Church had lots of interaction with other Episcopal churches. However, he could recall no contact or participation with other Italian Protestant churches. Abbate did recall quite clearly that his grandfather, Rev. Vasquez, who had studied for the priesthood in Rome, felt very offended when snubbed by Catholics.

Rev. Antonio Roca of Hartford's Italian Baptist Church, similarly, had plenty of contact with other area Baptist churches and pastors and frequently met and worked with other Italian Baptist ministers. Oftentimes the Italian ministers were outnumbered by Anglo-American preachers and in the *Hartford Courant* the latter received on these occasions more coverage than the former. For example, when Antonio Roca celebrated his ordination in Hartford, Rev. Ariel Bellondi attended and spoke, but so did Rev. Dr. Chivers, Dr. Stone, Rev. Thompson, Dr. Main, and Rev. Hastings. On April 29, 1903 the *Courant* noted that Bellondi preached on John 11:25, but summarized Dr. Chiver's charge in one full paragraph (5).

Christ for Hartford

In the *Baptist Home Mission Monthly* for December 190 cle titled "The Hartford Italian Mission" bears the byline Rev. Bruce, and yet almost all the words in the article are direct quotations from Rev. Roca. It is as if Rev. Bruce must be the filter or intermediary for Roca's words. Also, curious is the fact that if Italian Catholics did not like relegation by Irish Catholics to a church basement, then it may seem strange to enthuse about Italian Baptists in the "bright basement of the First Baptist Church" of Hartford (474).

In the February 4, 1909 issue of the *Watchman*, Hartford banker Charles E. Prior told the story of Roca's success as an evangelist, most notably by converting "an ordinary Italian," Antonio Granone, who then returned to Bisaccia, Italy, and started a Baptist church there (one that still exists today). Prior notes that after listening to Roca, Granone, on his return to Italy, "could never again countenance the idolatry, superstition and bondage of the Church of Rome" (10). Two years before in the *Watchman* (October 31, 1907), Dr. Stone referred to "the phenomenal success" of Roca's mission (21). The article has a large photograph of Stone, pastor of the Asylum Avenue Baptist Church in Hartford, but none of Roca.

Though Rev. De Carlo seems not to have visited or worked with the Baptist Italian Mission in Hartford, he had been a Baptist before becoming a Congregationalist, and later after leaving Hartford for Chicago he switched to Presbyterianism. When installed in Hartford, the *Courant* reported (July 9, 1903), De Carlo "presented his credentials, gave an account of his religious experiences and the reasons for his change of views" (7). De Carlo came to the United States from Calitri in 1888, and therefore his emigration preceded the time of Baptist awakening in this town, though perhaps there had already been some spiritual seed in the soil that accompanied him to Stamford, Connecticut, where he worked as a shoemaker and then as a self-taught evangelist. During his Chicago years, the Italian American poet Emanuel Carnevali briefly worked for him before moving on to a similarly brief stint with Harriet Monroe at *Poetry Magazine*. Although Carnevali wrote in his most famous poem "The Return," "Austria and the pope have gone their miserable way," he showed very little sympathy for his Presbyterian employer. Carnevali wrote in his *Autobiography*: De Carlo "had the face of a sour Presbyterian minister, which he was. His name was Pasquale and he was a shabby character, an ugly brute. [. . .] I never could imagine what kind of sermons he preached to his congregation. They must have been terrible if they resembled in any way their author's soul" (155).

Some twenty years prior in Hartford and before that in Stamford, the Italian community considered De Carlo one of their foremost leaders. It is true, too, that as an international modernist poet Carnevali most likely spoke for himself and not for a larger Italian-American community. At De Carlo's Hartford installation, Italian pastors had a significant role though once again they were outnumbered by Anglo-American ministers. Antonino Di Miceli led the opening prayer, Giuseppi Merlino read from Scripture, Joel S. Ives delivered a sermon in English, and Canio Cerreta of the Bridgeport Italian Congregational Church followed Ives with a sermon in Italian, and "nine Italian girls sang in English and a tenor solo was rendered by Mr. Sbrocco" (*Courant* July 9, 1903, 7). However, in addition to Ives the following Anglo or Scandinavian-American pastors and deacons attended, some with participatory roles: R. H. Potter, William Tucker, H. H. Kelsey, H. J. Gillette, Robert H. Wheeler, W. De Loss Love, Horace E. Mather, Joseph H. Twichell, Charles E. Thompson, S. K. Didrickson, S. E. Mac Geehon, Charles W. Crane, and Harry E. Peabody.

The Catholic lay-writer Thomas F. Meehan referred to such Protestant legions among the Italians as a "battalion of soul hunters" (19). Meehan wrote of New York City. What would he have found in Hartford circa 1903? In February of the following year, former city Alderman Olcott B. Colton delivered a lecture at the Asylum Hill Congregational Church titled "Hartford's East Side Populations." As reported in the *Courant* (February 15, 1904), Colton stated:

> There are approximately 4,000 Italians in Hartford, mostly of the lower classes, a few of the middle and none of the upper classes. Like the Jew, the Italian is a believer in large families. It is nothing uncommon for an Italian girl to marry at 14 and then one child a year may be added to the household. They live largely on a vegetable diet, and those who came from Italy are mostly of the agricultural class, and have had no opportunity to gain an education or to mingle with men. [. . .] They help one another in their poverty and are rather indifferent in religious matters, but are willing to adopt American customs. (6)

For a speaker such as Colton, these last listed characteristics were crucial: Italians were cooperative and not set in their ways and therefore they could be Americanized and the Congregational Church of Connecticut could be key in such work. "They are here to stay," Colton believed according to the *Courant*, "and we must make Americans of them" (6).

By 1915, according to the *Courant*, there were "12,000 people of Italian birth or descent" in the city and while there were "no Michel Angelos or Da Vincis in Hartford," the "ability and industry" of the Italian population "made them a very valuable part of the city's life" (August 29, 1915, X1). In fact, the *Courant* asserted that "because of the quickness with which the Italian assimilates American ideas and customs [. . .] few customs of the old country are retained and the 'quarter' is by no means a community in the sense that it is set off from other parts of the city by radical and sharply-drawn differences" (X1).

There were a number of concerns, however, including Italian anarchism and socialism, and for some a sense that this precious and unique state founded on Puritan principles had been inundated by a strange foreignness. When an organization called the Circle Libero Pensiero (Free Thought Circle) challenged the Italian Baptists and Italian Congregationalists to defend their principles, Rev. De Carlo met with them, but Rev. Roca did not. As reported in the *Courant* (October 24, 1910, 3), Roca noted that "when De Carlo [a few years prior] rose to defend the faith, such an uproar is said to have been made by the socialists that De Carlo was obliged to leave the hall." To Roca, the group's apparent leader, a photographer named Nunzio Vayana, had shown himself to be an atheist and an anarchist.

In 1911 "the leading Italians of Bristol" formed a benevolent society that in addition to aiding its members would "inculcate ideas of American citizenship" (*Courant* January 20, 1911, 15). Once in 1906 Rev. De Carlo went to Rocky Hill as a guest preacher. De Carlo spoke to a mixed audience of "Americans" and "Italians." The visit had been arranged by local minister Rev. Frank Waters and by "W. D. Manchester, manager of the Connecticut Trap Rock Quarry, where some forty Italians" worked (*Courant* March 6, 1906, 16). As reported: "during the services several familiar hymns were sung, Italian words being used." Was this special Sunday service not only an attempt to win souls for Christ, but also for America and for industrial management? Did the

Bristol benevolent society "inculcate ideas of American citizenship," in part, to ward off anarchistic ones?

Certainly there existed continuous fears that immigrant workers would go on strike at any moment and that America had already been lost. Rev. Ives reported at the seventy-ninth annual meeting of the Congregational Home Missionary Society "that Connecticut, like Massachusetts and Rhode Island had become a 'foreign state,' and that the percent of foreign parentage is rapidly increasing, because an increasing proportion of the large immigration locates in New England and because the birth rate of children of native parentage is smaller than the death rate" (*Courant* June 1, 1905, 5). In an essay of the same year, Ives reminded his fellow Congregationalists: "Connecticut has not been unmindful of her opportunity [. . .]" and "realizes that every Protestant enterprise must look to the alien for its maintenance and defense in the immediate future. The inbred Yankee," Ives warned, "is fast becoming a rarity" ("Italian Connecticut" 301).

During his keynote address for Connecticut's tercentenary celebration in 1935, Yale President James Rowland Angell depicted immigrants as a blight on a state that had moved too far from its roots. "'There have been very large invasions of foreign stock, to whom the traditional ideals of the Puritan are wholly alien [. . .],'" Angell told the crowd at the Bushnell Memorial in Hartford. While Angell expressed uncertainty regarding contemporary immigrants, even if "'these folks have become good and loyal citizens, furnishing an important part of the labor required by Connecticut industry,'" he had nothing but praise for the past, Connecticut's founders, and the characteristics of frugality and hard work (*Yale News* October 12, 1935, 1).

Rev. Ives believed that opportunity for evangelization and Americanization beckoned, the future for Ives seemed bright and promising and not overshadowed by an unmatchable past. "Here is a magnificent opportunity for Christian Missions," he proclaimed in 1908. "The material is right at hand" ("Italy in Connecticut" 607). Ives did not see a chasm between Yankee and immigrant. The Catholic priest Aurelio Palmieri, on the other hand, did not think Congregationalism could appeal to the Italian immigrant. According to Palmieri, Congregationalism's "complete doctrinal dissolution, and its lack of a central organization, exhaust its religious energies. Besides, its narrow nationalism and dry Puritan traditions, do not attract the sympathies of a foreign element" (186).

In Connecticut, and Hartford in particular, the Congregational Home Missionary Society had a history of service long before the time of Italian immigration. The Home Missionary Society began in 1816 "to assist congregations that are unable to support the gospel ministry and to send the gospel to the destitute within the United States" (*Courant* April 19, 1899, 5), and the City Missionary Society began in 1851 with the goal of spreading the gospel among foreign populations, establishing Sunday schools, assisting the poor, and raising funds for these purposes (*Courant* November 25, 1901, 1). At the state level, Rev. Ives reported in 1904 that the Missionary Society had established "twenty-two American, two Danish, one French, one German, and four Italian churches" (*Courant* March 7, 1904, 12). Ethnic churches for each ethnicity may have formed, and these churches usually had preachers from the particular ethnicity served; but on special occasions the ethnic pastor would be outnumbered by Anglo American preachers (indeed the local pastor may not have been the key speaker for the day), and rarely would an ethnic pastor serve in a regional association (unless it were one specifically for his ethnic group).

In 1912 there were 17,000 Protestant church members in Hartford and thirteen Congregational churches. The Methodists had seven, and others fewer than that number. Slightly more than 36 percent of church members were Congregationalists (*Courant* January 7, 1912, 10). In other words, both in the state and the city, Congregationalism remained a dominant force with one or more church in 167 out of 168 Connecticut towns or cities. West Haven became a separate town in 1921, forming the 169th town. Its First Congregational Church dates to 1719, and the church's current building to 1859.

During the fiftieth-anniversary celebration for the City Missionary Society, Rev. Merlino noted that his fellow Italians "were very poor, very ignorant, mentally, morally, and spiritually, and were much in need of religious education" (*Courant*, November 25, 1901, 10). Among the foreign populations and particular missions to each ethnic group, Italians would often be singled out and highlighted. For example, at a statewide Congregational conference in 1905, only "Italian Connecticut" had its own separate session (*Courant* October 18, 1905, 8). Italians were seen as an especially promising field and one reason, as noted previously, was the strongly held Protestant belief that Italians tended to be nominally Catholic at most—if they were Catholic at all. As the *Courant* noted in 1905, according to Rev. De Carlo, "there were 60,000

Italians in Connecticut and he was sure that not over 5,000 attended the Roman Catholic Church" (November 16, 1905, 14). Another reason for signaling the Italian population as special certainly had to have been what literary historian Richard Brodhead has called "the double dream of Italy" in America (1). According to Brodhead, the mind of one person could hold the strangely divergent views of Italy as the apotheosis of the Grand Tour and as the homeland of barbarian invaders overtaking America. On one occasion in 1904 at the Farmington Avenue Congregational Church, Rev. Ives spoke about missionary work in general and then Rev. De Carlo spoke about Italian "history and achievements" (*Courant* February 18, 1904, 3). On March 19, 1906 at Asylum Hill Congregational Church, F. Irwin Davis lectured on Italian art and culture (*Courant* 12). At the South Baptist Church that year, Miss C. Hewins's told her audience "tales of Italian travel" (*Courant* March 24, 1906, 11). In other words, for the elite of late nineteenth and early twentieth century Hartford, one went to Italy and Italians for the finest in the arts (even if other Italians were digging ditches for the new bridge across the Connecticut River). Poland was not such a paradise, and yet Polish and Italian immigrants both lived in tenement sections of Hartford and worked together at construction sites and on factory floors. During the celebration for the fiftieth anniversary of modern Italy at the Congregational Warburton Chapel, Rev. Willis H. Butler told the children of immigrants in the audience: "'You boys and girls have in you fine blood and behind you a great history. That history goes back to the early days of Rome,' he said: 'you bring here love of beauty and of art and of music'" (*Courant* September 20, 1920, 4). On the other hand, the *Courant* reported in 1904 that "a crowd of boys made trouble after the morning service [at the Italian Congregational Church] and it became necessary to station someone at each entrance to prevent them making a disturbance. Finally the police were appealed to [. . .]" (*Courant* March 28, 1904, 2).

The Warburton Chapel served as the second home for the Italian Congregational Church of Hartford. Its first home (1903–1907) had been at the Village Street Mission. After 1946, it used the Parker Memorial Chapel of Immanuel Congregational Church until September 1961, and then it moved to its final location, South Congregational Church. In other words, unlike the Bridgeport Italian Congregational Church, the Hartford one never had its own separate free-standing building, and unlike the Waterbury Church where Rev. Codella served as pastor for decades, before the long tenure of Rev. Ricciardi Hartford had six different pastors.

According to Hartford Congregational Church historian Robert Owen Decker, the Village Street Mission acted as a city institution and not a strictly denominational one. The mission had Baptist, Episcopal, and Methodist volunteers as well as Congregational ones (136–137). Though other ethnic groups participated in programs, the Mission's activities especially addressed the Italian population. In addition to the Mission, according to Decker, the neighborhood also had various distractions such as "poolrooms, movie houses, and dance halls [. . .]" (146). Even though (or perhaps because) Catholics "were urged by their church not to attend" Mission programs (150), the institution maintained its Italian focus for decades. For example, the eighty-eighth anniversary celebration for the City Missionary Society in 1939 began with an Italian dinner prepared by the Mothers' Club. "More than 100 persons paid fifty cents each for their Monday evening meal," Decker notes (151). Yet, the following year the Mission closed as the population served by it moved to other parts of the city (152). Similarly, Decker notes that after the Second World War "as the Italian population became more prosperous and more Americanized, they moved from the area, and a separate Italian ministry became less important" (236). Nonetheless, Rev. Ricciardi, as noted previously, continued to offer services in Italian at South Congregational for those who desired them well into the 1970s.

Decker observes that "persecution [of Italian Protestants] in Hartford came from many sides, not just from the Roman Catholic. The native American Protestant too often tended to see the Italian immigrant as socially inferior" (234). While the Congregational ministerial elite would never call Italian immigrants "socially inferior," they could at times be condescending or simply overwhelming. I also find it odd that while the Catholic approach to relegating Italians to the basement would receive criticism, the Protestant ministers did the same thing even if with welcome in their hearts instead of ridicule. As noted previously, the Italian pastors at Rev. De Carlo's installation could have easily felt submerged (or colonized) by the sheer number of Anglo-American pastors present (*Courant* July 9, 1903, 7).

Decker says Catholics and Native American Protestants could degrade Italian-American Protestants. But add to this the startling fact that sometimes even Italian Protestants might attack Italian Americans.

The *Courant* reported a talk by Mr. Pecorini of Venice delivered at the Hartford Seminary on October 24, 1903 (7). This visiting Waldensian, according to the *Courant*, claimed the Italian immigration "a menace" to America because in Italy "they were accustomed to consider all institutions of government hostile to the interests of the common people; so they still feel in America [. . .]." The social settlement, Pecorini believed, represented the main hope for the successful assimilation of Italian immigrants. Gino Speranza, on the other hand, reached the conclusion in the anti-immigrant early 1920s that not even the settlement approach could succeed in making Italians into Americans. As he concluded in *Race or Nation*, "We must abolish 'the immigrant' from our minds and from our lives; from our polity and from our policies" (254).

When a new Village Street Mission opened in 1904, a host of pastors and others spoke, and Rev. De Carlo seemed relegated to the end of a very long list of speakers (*Courant* April 23, 1904, 4). If the Mission meant to appeal to Italian immigrants, then perhaps Rev. De Carlo should have had a more prominent role that day. Five days later the *Courant* had a much longer article on the opening of the new Village Street Mission (April 28, 1904, 13). There were pictures of Col. Charles E. Thompson, Rev. W. De Loss Love, and Rev. Dr. E. P. Parker. There is no image of Rev. De Carlo. Parker's talk, in which he praises the interdenominational cooperation of the mission, has a full summary. According to the summary, Parker also stated the aim of the mission: " 'To bring some sunshine into their [the immigrants'] hearts and homes, to guard them against the perils which surround them, to give them some right views of life, to direct them into the ways and habits that will make them industrious, thrifty and virtuous men and women [. . .]' " (*Courant* April 28, 1904, 13). In such an environment, Parker observed, Jews " 'become nominal Christians' " and Catholics " 'become converted to Protestantism' " (*Courant* April 28, 1904, 13).

Such conversion—nominal or profound—could have clear advantages in early-twentieth-century Hartford. As local historian Tracey Wilson has written, "Travelers [insurance company] management, for example, only would hire young, single, white, Protestant, and native-born women" (40). So the young women of Hartford (such as Rev. William Zito's sister) born of Italian immigrant parents could work at the large insurance company if Protestant, but not if Catholic.

The Hartford Italian Congregational Church supported both Americanization *and* Italianization efforts. The church celebrated the Fourth of July, but also September 20 (a day to celebrate the unification of Italy) and Columbus Day. On Church anniversary days as well as the three holidays just mentioned (which can be categorized as American, Italian, and Italian American) hymns, patriotic songs, and opera excerpts were sung (in English and Italian). Mayor Henney of Hartford spoke at the 1905 September 20th celebration at the Italian Congregational Church, and after he finished "Miss Ruth Roberts began to sing in Italian, 'Addio Terra Navita'" (*Courant* September 25, 1905, 11). While the paper notes that Roberts "was very warmly received," it then says matter-of-factly, "The remainder of the music was by Vincenzo Sbrocco" (*Courant* September 25, 1905, 11). The paper offers no words of praise for Sbrocco.

The year before Mayor Henney and others offered the Italian Congregationalists congratulations on a successful first year. The *Courant* reported that the mayor "spoke of his pleasure in being present," and he informed the audience "that this was a grand country and a grand age and he urged his hearers to remember that they were Americans, to become citizens of the country and a part of the country" (*Courant* July 18, 1904, 7). Similarly another speaker, Olcott B. Colton, "spoke of the connection between church membership and Christianity and American citizenship" (*Courant* July 18, 1904, 7). Yet all these celebratory occasions also fostered some sense of *italianità*. These new Americans were or would become also Italian Americans. And so when the festivities came to an end that day everyone sang "America" but *in Italian* for some (as printed in the program) and in English for others.

And when the congregation celebrated Italian identity they praised the Risorgimento and nationalism, not an individual home or ancestral town, not *campanilismo*. For example, when the Hartford Italian Congregational Church celebrated the thirty-fourth anniversary of Italian unification "the hall," according to the *Courant* (September 19, 1904, 4), "was filled, floor and galleries, and was decorated with Italian colors, and flags and banners of Italy and the United States. At the back of the platform were portraits of Washington, Lincoln and Roosevelt and the Italian heroes, Mazzini, Joseph Garibaldi, King Victor Emmanuel [. . .]." A band played selections from Verdi's operas and all was "patriotic" and "enthusiastic." Rev. Dr. Parker delivered the address in which he praised "Count Cavour who made the Italy of today" and extolled the "improvement of Italy since 1870, her development in art, the sciences, letters, manufacturing and agriculture, and all that pertains in the welfare of the nation" (*Courant* September 19, 1904, 4).

A decade later the Italian Church celebrated the forty-fourth anniversary of modern Italy. Almost two-hundred people, according to the *Courant*, attended and in the chapel "'Old Glory' and the Italian flag were stationed opposite each other [. . .]" (September 21, 1914, 15).

After the Second World War, Rev. Natale Ricciardi journeyed to Italy, and after six months returned to Hartford. He, too, reported on progress and democracy when he spoke to one-hundred people at Immanuel Congregational Church. The *Courant* report concludes, "Scores of Hartford persons received messages from relatives in Italy through Rev. Mr. Ricciardi" (September 28, 1948, 6). In other words, Americanization (and the Second World War) still did not mean total loss of either Italian identity or identification with and concern for one's ancestral or native land.

John Foster Carr noted in his 1911 *Guide to the Immigrant Italian*, published under the auspices of the Connecticut Daughters of the American Revolution, that "you cannot be in America a single day without understanding the necessity of speaking the same language [English] that all other men in America speak" (14–15), and yet even before Carr's writing virtually every mission to Italians instituted classes in Italian as well as English. While it may be true that some Italian immigrant parents wanted their children to speak only English in hope of advancing their progress in America, a countertrend was to maintain some connection to ancestral culture through Italian language classes. While Mayor Henney speaking at the Italian Congregational Church in 1905 "urged the parents to talk English at home as much as possible [. . .]" (*Courant* July 24, 1905, 4), Rev. Rose in 1920 promoted Italian language classes for the immigrant children of Hartford (Decker 235). Rev. Zito told me that he and his siblings could understand their parents when they spoke Italian, but the children were not encouraged to learn or to speak it.

William Abbate told me that his grandfather, Rev. Vasquez, offered social support as well as spiritual leadership for the members of Saint Paul's Italian Episcopal Church. Rev. Vasquez, he said, had phenomenal language skills and assisted neighbors whether or not they attended his church. At least from the Congregational or Episcopal view, this local social support in conjunction with or even separate from religious activity distinguished these churches from Catholic ones.

For example, in April 1908 the *Courant* reported that Congregational minister Pietro F. Vodola "tramped the streets" with a young Italian man of Hartford "till dinner time, trying to get him work. Factories, stores and individuals were visited, at each place the pastor acting as spokesman" (April 25, 1908, 4). And contrastingly in one of his short stories, early-twentieth-century Italian American writer Giuseppe Cautela describes a child's death and the funeral that followed and how a Catholic priest wanted "'ten dollars for the blessing of the body'" and the narrator of the story says to the boy's uncle, "'Consider this a piece of business like any other and let it go at that'" (203). In other words, these various narratives perpetuated a belief that Protestant ministers aided life in the new American world, while Catholic priests were difficult obstructionists as they had been back in Italy (and here in America these priests did not even speak Italian).

The ministers of the Hartford Italian Congregational Church were Italians who spoke Italian to Italians. They also did what they could to find work for their members and to foster their members' English language skills. They distributed Bibles and encouraged literacy. They believed that not only did literacy provide a path to success in America but also a more direct experience of Christ, and one based on a conscious individual choice. Below is a list of these ministers and their dates of service:

> Pasquale R. De Carlo, 1903–1906
> Pietro F. Vodola, 1906–1912
> Vincenzo Solimene, 1913–1918
> Philip M. Rose, 1919–1925
> Domenic D'Addario, 1926–1930
> Piero Chiminelli, 1931–1936
> Natale Ricciardi, 1937–1976

Rev. Chiminelli, before coming to Hartford, had "held pastorates in Rome, Naples and Florence, Italy" (*Courant* May 22, 1931, 28). Rev. Ricciardi came to Hartford following seven years at the New Britain, Connecticut Italian Congregational Church. At his welcoming reception Italian Americans had a larger role than the Anglo American elite. Phelps, Hooker, Potter, and English came, but only as "invited guests."

Interestingly, Professor Louis H. Naylor of Trinity College spoke and showed "Italian pictures" (*Courant* February 2, 1937, 20). Rev. Ricciardi preached in Connecticut for forty-six years and even at the age of seventy-five expressed his reluctance to retire. As the *Courant* reported in May 1976, there are "still a few old-timers who need his help" (May 1, 1976, 19). The paper said that up until the 1960s were "years when Italian immigrants and their children needed support—religious and social—and many were hard-pressed to function in an English speaking society" (*Courant* May 1, 1976, 19). The *Courant* added that according to Pastor Ricciardi, "As the Italian population around Hartford became more prosperous and more assimilated, the Italian ministry became less important" (19).

Rev. Ricciardi himself moved to Goose Hill Road in Chester, Connecticut. Born in Patti, Italy in 1900, he came to the United States in 1920. He was eighty-three when he died, and his funeral took place at the Deep River, Connecticut Baptist Church (*Courant* April 14, 1984, B8).

In the early years of the twentieth century, religion had been prominent in the news, covered at length, and often featured on the front page. Yet, by the end of the century such news—like Rev. Ricciardi's obituary—received less reportage and moved further away from prominence. Consider this brief notice from the *Springfield Republican*, July 13, 1910: "Rev. and Mrs. Alfred Barone of East Hartford, Connecticut are visiting friends in" Monson (10). Even a minister's movements it seems had some importance then, and although I had no idea that my great-grandfather and great-grandmother ever called East Hartford home, I am sure that Alfredo and Rosina Barone would have agreed with Rev. Ives: "let the Gospel Trumpet blow a final blast. The Gospel is the POWER OF GOD UNTO SALVATION to the Italian, the Hun and the Slav, as truly as to the Puritan and the Pilgrim" ("Gospel" 333).

Chapter 7

A Sermon for the Oppressed

"After we lost our money Mother took to New Thought and wouldn't have it that there was such a thing as death."

—Evelyn Waugh, *The Loved One*

Evangelization

In the early 1870s nearly 10,000 Americans visited Florence, Italy annually. The American Church of this city sought to meet the spiritual needs of such guests whether they attended Baptist, Congregational, Episcopal, Methodist, Presbyterian, or Reformed services at home. This effort began in 1861, under the care of a New York City–based advisory board. But immediately the Florence Church undertook mission activities for the Italian population through its schools, orphan asylum, and charity fund. After ten years of ministering to the needs of American visitors and Italian residents, Rev. Dr. Abraham Rynier Van Nest delivered a sermon interestingly titled—since he was a Protestant preaching in Catholic Italy—"The Holy Catholic Church." A note precedes the published text indicating that "many requests were made for its publication," and that the sermon presents "the principles, on which our Church is founded [. . .]." In this sermon Rev. Van Nest spoke on I Corinthians 12:28: "And God hath set some in the church"—reasoning that this is one of the few references to a church in scripture, whereas there are so many references to Christ. "Some preachers [. . .]," he says, "instead of directing souls to the Saviour and his atonement [. . .] point them to the church and its sacraments [. . .]" (3). This, according to Van Nest, is a mistake. He then sets out to prove his point through an examination of Jewish and Christian history, moving from "a dispensation of severity, to one of grace" (6).

Van Nest then notes that Jesus actually gave us "no authority in any express saying from his lips" regarding any church. "The only time, when he spoke at any length of the Church, is recorded in 18th chapter of St. Matthew; where he dilates upon its solemn powers and says, 'where two or three are gathered together in my name, there am I in the midst of them'" (6). A church then is any gathering of people in Christ's name. Faith, baptism, and communion are all that such a gathering requires for those are the only necessities of which Christ spoke. Christ is primary; any church, secondary. "Any form" for a church according to Van Nest, "is good that conduces to the order and comfort of the house of God." He continues, "All Churches are true; whether Congregational, Presbyterian or Episcopalian, so long as they hold the essential principles, on which the Church is built; faith in Christ and an observance of his [two] sacraments" (7).

Up to this point Rev. Van Nest has used the word *Catholic* only in his title. But one follows easily the loud sounds of his silences. There is a Church that sees the Church institution and not Christ's spirit as primary. There is a church that has heaped on its members extra-scriptural sacraments and rituals. But near the end he addresses what has only been implicit. "There is scarcely a term so perverted as this word 'Catholic,'" he says (9).

Americans in Florence comprised the audience for Van Nest's sermon. He warned his listeners to give, "the hand of fellowship to all" and "far distant be the day, when Americans in Europe shall set the example of divisions in the body of Christ," but he meant only Protestant Americans for those who call themselves Catholic have "shut themselves up in a dark corner of Christendom" (9).

Antonio Mangano, born in one of those "dark corners"—Acri, Italy—in 1869, came to the United States as a young boy, attended Colgate Academy, Colgate, Brown, and Columbia Universities, and Union Theological Seminary. He believed that preachers attempting to evangelize Italians should not denigrate the Catholic Church. Such a preacher, Mangano believed, should be familiar with both Catholic and Protestant beliefs. He said, "In presenting the message to a non-Protestant audience, it is essential that a man shall draw comparisons between the two systems, but such comparison should be made in a conciliatory manner" (*Religious Work* 23). Vehement attacks on Catholicism, he added, do "not make indifferent Catholics favorable to the Protestant position" (*Religious Work* 23). Mangano also argued that the evangelical missionary should be familiar with the "content of socialism as well as with the utterances of the materialistic philosophers" (*Sons of Italy* 183).

As important as a preacher's rhetorical content or his required store of knowledge is his mode of speaking; a discourse's method of appeal. Against the stereotype that Italians are an emotional people, Mangano suggested that pastors address the intellect of their congregants. "One of the things that we have learned by experience," he observed, "is that, while there is power in the emotional appeal, it is the appeal that is made to the intellect that wins the allegiance of the Italians" (*Sons of Italy* 184).

Anglo American Baptist minister Edwin P. Farnham cited Mangano's life as evidence to "assure all doubters that the processes of industrial, educational, social, moral and American evolution that have produced for us this specimen of a cultivated Christian gentleman are entirely capable of doing the same thing over and over again" (315). Mangano, this paragon of rational American conditioning, delivered a commencement address at Brown University in 1899. In this twelve-page handwritten oration, he began with a proposition regarding American expansionism. He asked should the United States "embark upon a policy of expansion, and endeavor to spread their civilization and beneficent institutions among benighted peoples, or should they, after forcing the Spanish rule from Cuba, Porto-Rico [sic], and the Philippines, leave these semi-barbarous peoples to their own fate and attend strictly to home affairs?" (1). Mangano, in classical oration form, next narrates the different views expressed on this question. He concludes, "Whether you agree or disagree with the Expansion policy does not in the least alter the situation [. . .] we have already expanded [. . .]" (2–3). Therefore, he adds, what really matters is how the United States meets "new responsibilities" (3).

He offers four proofs for the moral necessity of involvement with these territories. To ignore them, he says, would be purely "mercenary," and instead the United States must demonstrate to the world that "wherever the stars and stripes are found, there is also found, the school-house, religious freedom, and the fruits of American civilization"

(4–5). Mangano warns that no spoil system should be put in place, but there must be "local self-government" (7). He notes that "the peoples of our new dependencies cannot leap in a single day from absolute barbarism to the most perfect Anglo-Saxon civilization" (8). This is an interesting assertion. Just as the Italian can be Americanized, the Filipino may be civilized and the measure for both Americanization and civilization is the Anglo-Saxon-Protestant yardstick. Mangano believes neither the immigrant nor the island "barbarian" are representative of what many of his contemporaries called hopeless "inferior stock." He did think that the United States could grant others "every opportunity for development" (8). At the same time that Mangano endorses "the ultimate independence of our new possessions" (9), he also refers to the peoples of these lands as "child races" (10). He concludes the body of his oration as follows: "Ethically then, it is demanded of us that we govern these peoples with the noblest motives, and that we prepare them as speedily as possible for self-government" (10). If this effort succeeds, he announces in his peroration, then "the oppressed everywhere shall look to you [America] for deliverance" (12).

Mangano's student commencement speech allows us to see his mind in its development. He did take several trips to Italy to improve his skills in his native language, to study, and to evangelize, but his attitude toward himself as well as toward Italians and Italian Americans resembled his attitude regarding the peoples of the new United States territorial possessions. He had a colonizer's attitude, even if a kindhearted one. Farnham notes in his brief portrait of Mangano:

> Young Mangano was a stripling of about ten years when he was received in the country home of Mr. and Mrs. Robert E. Dietz at Hempstead, Long Island. Here he toiled industriously for ten full years, winning the confidence and affection of his employers, who are swift to testify their appreciation of his efficiency and unfailing integrity. (315)

Mangano, Farnham adds, "is the natural product of good environment" (315). In Farnham's perfectly reasonable turn-of-the-century Darwinism, had this "good environment" perhaps superseded the inferior inherited traits of a Southern Italian? Mangano named his Brooklyn Church not after his Italian parents or Christopher Columbus, but after his Hempstead, Long Island employers: the Dietz Memorial (the Dietz family made the largest monetary contribution to this church).

Late in the twentieth century, Rev. Arthur Caliandro worked for years under the tutelage of one of America's most famous ministers, Norman Vincent Peale. But Arthur's father, Tomasso, had also been a minister. How did Caliandro balance the influence of his famous mentor and his "fiery" Italian-Methodist father?

Mangano endorsed a rational speaking style and downplayed emotional appeals. Is this true for other Italian American preachers? From the earliest periods, Protestant sermons have been a staple of the American literary and political scene. How do the sermons preached in Italian American Protestant Churches or by Protestant Italian-Americans in mainline Protestant churches conform to or differ from traditional Protestant sermons, and what does this suggest about the nature of American identities? We have already seen that Mangano's commencement oration follows a standard form (though one could say the form originates in Cicero and Quintilian), and he seems to have heavily accentuated Americanization though not entirely forsaking his *italianità*.

Since Protestant faiths emphasize textual analysis, it seems odd that little of the writing that has been done on the subject of Italian Protestants studies the actual preaching of ministers. One possible explanation for this historical lacuna is that not many of these sermons survive, and second, of those that survive some are in Italian (which may pose a challenge to their analysis for the American scholar). On the other hand, church records for Italian American Protestant congregations survive all across the country. Could this be so because the Italian church often had an Anglo American committee of oversight and so these records, their perpetuation, demonstrate the Anglo American elite's benevolence and their leadership while an Italian minister's sermons might reveal his leadership and perhaps his independence?

Nonetheless, there are many comments in spiritual autobiographies and elsewhere regarding the art of preaching. There remain various plans for the education of preachers. And, of course, there are some sermons.

How did a minister appeal to his auditors? The debate regarding appeals to the heart or to the intellect has been a long-lasting one in American Protestantism. In the Great Awakening of the mid-eighteenth-century Presbyterian Gilbert Tennent proclaimed in his most famous sermon, *The Danger of an Unconverted Ministry*, that the "Prayers and Preachings" of unawakened ministers were "both dead as a Stone" (7). Yet, elsewhere he said that "proffering the Passions before the Understanding & Judgment in religious matters is Foolish, Dangerous, Unjust, Undecent, Brutish, & Diabolical" ("Thoughts on extempore Preaching"). Tennent claimed that appeals to both the intellect and the passions were necessary for effectual preaching. Two considerations were the spiritual state of the speaker and the nature of his audience. He emphasized spontaneity and emotion when addressing farmers such as in his lengthy *A Solemn Warning to the Secure World*, and was more rational and concise when addressing fellow Presbyterian ministers such as in *The Blessedness of Peace-Makers*. When he addressed an audience of both parishioners and preachers, as on the day he preached *The Danger of an Unconverted Ministry*, he would be concise but make use of emotional appeals.

Consideration of an audience's nature as well as the appropriateness of concision or expansion and the appropriateness of emotional or intellectual appeals were matters of great importance to the Italian Protestant ministers. As we have already seen, Mangano recommended thoughtfulness and not accusation when addressing a Catholic audience and reason and not emotion when addressing Italians. George Broadman Taylor, longtime leader of the American Baptist missionaries in Italy, advocated a balance between passion and reason. He wrote:

> Some sermons would be improved were there less going after originality and more effort to simply find and present the thought of the Holy Spirit in the passage selected. In the latter, at least, there is ample scope for the creative faculty. Some discourses, on the other hand, fail for lack of life and color. After all, if a preacher is not interesting enough to induce people to listen to him, his 'best laid plans' and most logically constructed trains of thought are in vain. (*Life and Letters* 259–260)

Despite the teachings of such leaders of the Italian missionary movement as Antonio Mangano and George Boardman Taylor, there were Italian pastors who accentuated emotional appeals. A member of the Milwaukee Italian Evangelical Church recalls that its pastor, August Giuliani, "'was very theatrical and when he would give his sermon, it was a lesson in drama. He'd make you cry, he'd make you laugh'" (Tanzilo 221). Lewis Turco told me that his father's "subjects were pretty standard, but sometimes he'd become so engrossed or involved with what he was saying that he would begin to weep in the pulpit, which made me squirm" (Letter).

Other appeals a pastor might make would be through brevity or length, timeliness of topic, location outside the church building, and even use of technology. Taylor, late in life—1906, preached in Rome on the 90th Psalm. He wrote, "[. . .] which I did for fourteen minutes, as it is a psalm by me much studied and meditated, and greatly loved" (*Life and Letters* 347). On the other hand, when Angelo di Domenica preached in Italy after the Second World War he "preached for nearly two hours in every service" (*Protestant Witness* 161). These sermons, though, seemed to have been propaganda for the United States as much as for Christ. Di Domenica recalls, "First of all, I spoke about America and the contribution Italy made toward her greatness [. . .]" (161). Interestingly, in speaking to Italian Protestants he evoked solidarity for their struggles during the Fascist era. "I was aware of their persecution in Italy, so I told them that in America we knew about it. I said that they were not alone [. . .]" (162). He says that he avoided any talk of material conditions—American wealth and Italian poverty—for he did not want to depress his auditors. Then, he writes, "having given them general information about America, the rest of the time was devoted to giving them a simple message of the gospel" (162). He is rather vague and imprecise here in his memoir. How much time did he devote to America? How much to the gospel?

Angelo di Domenica suggested that sermons be timely. In his autobiography he tells that during the Second World War he preached twenty-one "War Time Sermons." He provides a list noting title and text. Number one: "God Bless America—We are proud to be Americans. Psalm 33:12" (147). Number eight: "The Acceptance of a Draftee. Gal. 1:15; Acts 26:19" (147). And so on.

Another means to spread the gospel was the outdoor or tent meeting. Di Domenica recalls that at his Philadelphia church on South Broad Street there was an empty lot. He held open-air services there during which he incorporated the latest technology. As he recalled in the mid-fifties looking back at the mid-teens: "I illustrated my talks with religious stereopticon views" (69). What follows in *Protestant Witness* is most interesting for it raises the question: what is most effective in attracting possible converts? Is it the traditional text, doctrine, reason, use sermon? Di Domenica recalls, "By chance, a woman passed and was attracted by the pictures I was showing. She came inside of the iron fence of the lot and listened with devotion to my explanation of the pictures" (69). But note that the pictures first attracted this Philadelphian, not the preacher's words. (And today one can purchase well-produced DVDs of Rev. Caliandro preaching at Marble Collegiate Church or read his sermons on-line at the Church's website.)

In Hartford De Carlo's successor at the Italian Congregational Church improvised a unique version of the outdoor meeting or service. Rev. Vodola preached each Sunday afternoon in the summer at three o'clock "from a gospel wagon at the corner of Front and Kilbourn streets" (*Courant* July 4, 1908, 4). He would pass out cards at the close of his sermon with a message in Italian to those who desired "to lead better lives." Anyone interested would sign the card and return it to Rev. Vodola who would personally meet with each of those persons later in the week.

Another aspect of open-air evangelization would be the work of colporteurs. During August of 1902 Rev. Mazzuca (Baptist) preached in a New Haven, Connecticut park. During these Sundays "tracts, New Testaments and Bibles" were distributed ("Italians—New Haven, Conn."). Oftentimes, converts record that reading the Bible or hearing music (or seeing stereopticon views) first led to their interest in a Protestant church.

Institutionalization

During the intensely active years of foreign missions, churches also answered a need and an opportunity to evangelize among the immigrants that came to America. If the years following 1860 were a time to reach Italians in Italy, the years near the turn of the century initiated an effort to minister to Italian immigrants. Mangano warned that in order to adapt Italians to American customs, Americans themselves must change their attitudes regarding Italian immigrants. In 1917 he wrote:

> Outside of pastors and settlement or lay workers, who come in close contact with Italians and both respect and love them, the ordinary American dislikes, distrusts, fears, and shuns Italians, noticing only their external dirt, the smell of garlic, and the picturesque violent crimes committed by their black sheep. (*Religious Work* 18)

These attitudes—pro-immigrant or anti-immigrant—impacted immigrant church structure. Looking back over the years of the Italian Baptist Church in Philadelphia from the vantage point of 1948, Angelo di Domenica recalled that the Philadelphia church began its work in 1891 and none other than world famous preacher Russell H. Conwell provided a salary for Antonio Pinto, the church's first missionary. Rev. Alberto Chiera after the turn of the century received support from the American Baptist Publication Society and the Woman's Auxiliary. When Rev. di Doemnica arrived in 1914, he worked toward securing a permanent home and structure which the Baptist Union purchased for the Italian Church in 1921. Di Domenica also thanked volunteer workers such as Miss Ethel Downsbrough, Mr. Lynn K. Lewis, Mr. Emmet R. Shephard, and Miss Elizabeth Robinson ("St. John's Baptist Church" 31–32). In other words, even in a branch ethnic church there could be much reliance on and interaction with Anglo-centered congregations.

Mangano believed such a branch church, such as di Domenica's Philadelphia one, the best way to organize an Italian church. In *Sons of Italy* he outlined several modes of organization for these young churches: departmental, branch, and self-governing or fully independent. The first occurred when an established church set aside a room for Italian evangelization and paid for the support of this work (167). A branch church with its own building, Mangano said, "has been found to accomplish the best result" (168). A fully self-governed church, according to Mangano, had its own building and pastor, but had to bear full responsibility for the support of both as well as any missionary work that the church may undertake. A branch church could receive not only outside financial help, but Italians could benefit from the experience of more established Americans and Americans could get to know Italian immigrants. If there is cooperation between an immigrant congregation and an established nearby one, then, according to Mangano:

> There are two very important ends served by this arrangement. It is a protection against ill-advised action on the part of the Italian congregation, and at the same time it provides a means whereby our American friends can better understand Italian problems and views and more fully sympathize with the Italian temperament. (175)

As he so frequently did, Mangano tried to negotiate a middle ground. His position indicated that Italians needed "protection," but also that Americans needed a lesson in toleration. He concluded here with the altruistic wish that "both sides would learn to respect, love, and help each other more, as they thus become acquainted" (175).

At nearly the same time, schools for Italian Baptist ministers formed in Rome and New York. At the start of the twentieth century the American Baptist mission organized a Theological School with the goal of increasing the number of native Italian pastors. Taylor noted in his 1902 mission report, "To the organizing of the new Theological School in Rome I gave my best efforts [. . .]" He had various concerns, especially financial. "The field here is wide," he reported, "and in some respects inviting, but to what extent will there be means of supporting in the work the young men who year after year will be going forth from the school?" Perhaps Taylor had no need for concern for the number of students would remain small. Rev. Dexter Whittinghill noted in the same yearly report that the school had a faculty of four (in addition to Taylor and Whittinghill, Henry Paschetto, and N. H. Shaw) and six students. These six studied the Bible, Systematic Theology and Ethics, Church History, Ecclesiology, Apologetics, Pastoral Theology, Hebrew, Greek, English, Elocution, Vocal Music, and Homiletics. Occasional lectures on Sociology and Christian Archaeology were also provided. Whittinghill asserted, "We expect to insist on a high standard of work from the beginning, for it will be impossible for our students to contend with a system so old and subtle as the Papacy without a thorough preparation in mind and heart." Five years later there were ten students. Whittinghill said in the 1907 report: "Three years are required to finish the course of study. The greatest need in our Mission is pious men, called of God to preach the gospel."

A curious surviving two-page handwritten in English manuscript of Rev. Barone's is "The Requirements necessary for the ministry's candidate examination." Perhaps this difficult to read list of twelve items—often further subdivided—had been prepared for Francesco Sannella. The list contains some similarities to the Baptist schools in Rome and, as we shall see, in New York. Barone lists for example at number two: "Perfect knowledge of the Bible." Barone however includes, number six, "the Philosophical doctrine," and then follows a long list ranging from Aristotle to Machiavelli. Number twelve one might call a bit of practical education: "Two years of ministry's practice." And then follows the most unique item of all—"Second the Knowledge of Rev. Alfred Barone—pastor."

The Italian Department of Colgate University began in 1907 at 79 Hewes Street, Brooklyn under the direction of Rev. Antonio Mangano. Other instructors that first year included Rev. Lewis Scelfo, Rev. James M. Bruce, and Miss M. E. Gordon ("Italian Theological School"). The three-year course of study included "a Systematic study of the whole Bible, courses in church history, English and Italian languages, New Testament Greek, theology, homiletics with weekly exercises in preaching, and a considerable experience on various mission fields" (Mangano, *Religious Work* 18). It is interesting to note that the list does not include a course in American history or civics as might be expected during an assimilationist period in history, though it does appear that Mangano added such a course later; perhaps in reaction to fervent anti-immigration thought.

Twenty years later, "A School of Prophets," a tribute to Rev. Mangano, opened with a fanciful dialogue between Italian Baptist ministers planning for a future school. The character in the play "Rev. Ariel Bellondi" says that at the seminary envisioned for the near-future students will "receive a training in the elements of the Bible, Church History, Preaching and in the English and Italian languages" (1). Later the play notes that by 1928, forty-four "young men have received proper Christian training in our school" and out of that number all but three of them "have proven to be good and faithful ministers of the Gospel among their countrymen [. . .]" (11). The play ends with optimism as the spirit Genius proclaims, "Think of the future which is ahead of you. In the next 20 years you shall be able to accomplish more, very much more" (12).

Alas, such future achievements were not to be obtained by the Italian Department of Colgate. Some few years later, Rev. Mangano announced "The Closing of The Italian Department." This eight-page typed report includes the origins of the school, describes its program, and outlines changes in the world that render its closing necessary. Of the students Mangano wrote:

> The students who were admitted into our Department during the past twenty four [sic] years were not all of the same grade intellectually. Some had had an equivalent to our High school and even a college course. The larger part

> of our young men however came from the group whose educational advantages had been limited. Some could speak a little English—others could not form a sentence correctly in the English language—while still others knew their native tongue very imperfectly. But they all had a genuine missionary fervor, and had an earnest desire to lead their fellow-countrymen to a knowledge of Christ. These we received and gave to them the best we had. (3)

In 1932, however, this Italian Department in the American evangelical tradition that places conversion ("genuine missionary fervor") before and above education (which is not to say education has no value), closed its doors to any additional entrants.

Among the reasons given for this closure are "restricted immigration," "improved living conditions," the distractions of a consumer culture, and changes in the Italian nation. Mangano observed that since Mussolini's rise to power, "Unusual efforts have been put forth by the Italian government to keep the Italians all over the world united to Italy. The government feels that the Catholic church is of great assistance in its aims and so backs it with money and law" (5). As noted previously, although Mangano recommended the closing of the theology school, he also proposed that the ethnic church still had its purpose in America, especially for outreach to young people, strengthening of family ties, convenience of neighborhood location, and understanding of "the mental process of the Italian of the second and third generation [. . .]" (7).

∼

As early as 1917, Mangano had divided religious work among Italians in America into three stages. The first stage according to Mangano was a period of experimental evangelization, roughly 1880 to 1900. The second stage was one of "permanent work," or what I have called "institutionalization": a period "marked by the erection of special buildings," formulation of policies, and "the matter of training schools for the preparation of workers [. . .]" (*Sons of Italy* 163–164). Mangano called his third stage the "intensive" one. A continuation of already existing efforts with an eye to greater efficiency, this stage looked to the future. I will use the word *transformation* for a third stage that follows the "permanent work" or institutionalization. This transformation has its origins in events of the late 1920s and early 1930s, but accelerates after the end of World War II. Mangano had said in "The Closing of the Italian Department" that "the omnipresent moving picture theatre has militated against our work" (4) and at almost the same time Rev. Vasquez at Saint Paul's Italian Episcopal Church in Hartford asked in a sermon, "What do we see every day in this our beloved city? The majority of people 'go after' pleasures, forgetting the purpose of our spiritual life. Temptations for young and old" (*Courant* April 22, 1929, 3). What Vasquez sensed may have been postponed by global depression and global conflict, but many observers saw a purposelessness in the American prosperity of the postwar boom.

The authors of *The Split-Level Trap* (1960) rhetorically asked near the start of their examination of affluent suburbs, which they renamed "disturbia": "Why do we needle the typical American about his shiny mass-produced house and car, his manners and mores?" The answer: "Possibly because he represents the great sad joke of our time. Having amassed a wealth that used to be the subject of fairy tales, he often finds that he isn't happy after all. Somewhere, something is missing" (20). Could that missing factor be faith? Rev. Norman Vincent Peale, Caliandro's mentor, published his hugely popular *The Power of Positive Thinking* (1952) nearly a decade before the Bergen County, New Jersey case-studies of *The Split-Level Trap*. Rev. Peale offered simple solutions for complex problems, solutions rooted in popular psychology and popular religion. Perhaps that was the essence of his appeal. To the frazzled suburbanite he offered advice such as: "To have a mind full of peace merely fill it full of peace" (20), and "The secret of a better and more successful life is to cast out those old, dead, unhealthy thoughts. Substitute for them new, vital, dynamic faith thoughts" (172).

Gordon, Gordon, and Gunther, though, tell in *The Split-Level Trap* the story of a young Italian American woman who in her move from the city across the river to the suburbs has become unmoored and perhaps the power of positive thinking would not be power enough for Gina Conning. "Gina and John Conning," we're told, "came into Bergen County during the mid-1950s, full of hope for a bright future" (50). Their marriage was an exogamous one and they had many cultural chasms besides religion to bridge. Gina came from a New York City Italian Catholic working-class family. Her family shouted. John came from a Protestant suburban family and his dad owned Conning

Sheet Metal, Inc. They whispered. According to the authors, "John's parents saw Gina and people of her national, religious and economic background as intruders from below [. . .]" (53). Confronting difficulty adjusting to marriage, motherhood, and life in the suburbs, and not knowing where else to turn when particularly agitated one night, Gina runs "in the small dark hours of a snowy morning" to the local police station so that she does not harm her husband or child with a knife (50). Parenthetically, the authors observe: "(A woman of middle-class American Protestant ancestry, caught in Gina's kind of situation, might more typically have been afraid of poisoning or suffocating loved ones than of stabbing them)" (64), a parenthetical thought that perpetuates a long-standing anti-Italian stereotype. Like Rev. Peale, these authors, too, offer relatively simple, catchphrase solutions. Instead of "positive thinking," Gordon, Gordon, and Gunther suggest "compromise." John and his dad will meet halfway in their visions for the family company. John's mom and his wife will enjoy serving their husbands a veal scaloppini dinner (254). For the Connings all in "disturbia" will be restored to calm.

Transformation

During the turbulent times of the fabulous fifties, Rev. Luigi Turco underwent a spiritual crisis, a crisis rooted in changing demographic fact. Born in Riesi, Sicily in 1890, he came to America as a young man and found the American Catholic Church to be in control of the Irish and hence unwelcoming. Episcopalians converted him but Turco found them inhospitable to Italians as well and, therefore, he joined with the many Italians who had become Baptists. Beginning in the fall of 1919, he attended Rev. Mangano's Italian Department of Colgate Theological Seminary. He recalls in "A Brief Story of My Life":

> The school took Italian immigrants who had been converted here from Catholicism to Protestantism. Practically all the students were men over twenty years of age with little education, so in the school the Italian and English languages were studied; an elementary American history, an elementary church history and theology; now and then some prominent man gave us a lecture on various subjects. I had gone to

grammar school in Italy, and I was considered one of the best intellectual students, so one may see that at the end of the course the men were not well prepared for the work of the ministry. (5)

From the fall of 1924 through the spring of 1925 his cohort along with Rev. Mangano went to the Waldensian Seminary in Rome. Turco also visited Riesi during this time. After his return to the US, he served as pastor for two Italian Baptist congregations in Buffalo, New York for seventeen years; and then as pastor of the Italian Baptist Church of Meriden, Connecticut for sixteen years, 1938–1954. During the early 1950s his Meriden congregation decided they needed a younger preacher and they needed to Americanize the church. Turco recalls, "considering the scarcity of Italian churches and my age, it would have been difficult to find another church" ("Brief Story" 8).

In "distress one night" ("Brief Story" 8) he began reading Thomas Troward's *Bible Mystery and Bible Meaning*. He found his reading difficult, but reassuring: "God was disintegrating me in order to integrate me," he concluded ("Brief Story" 8). He stayed up all night reading and the next day ordered more books by Troward. He felt that for the next two years his "preaching was more vigorous and enthusiastic [. . .]" ("Brief Story" 9). He then read the writings of Mary Baker Eddy (Christian Scientist). He had "more vigor and enthusiasm for the work of the church," yet, nonetheless, he "had to resign the first of July, 1954" at age sixty-four ("Brief Story" 9).

He returned again to family in Riesi. While in Italy, he received a call to assume the pastorate of St. John the Baptist Church in the Bronx, New York. He accepted the position and while at this church he tried to broaden its base beyond the Italian community, and he continued his reading in contemporary theology. The works of Ernest Holmes "elated" him ("Brief Story" 12). But his family remained in Meriden and the old members of his new congregation did not like his outreach to the African American community. As Lewis Turco recalled:

> He had taken the Bronx assignment because the church there was dying because the Italian community was disappearing and a Black one emerging. As always, my father refused to bow to fate, and he went out to recruit Black families for his congregation. That was okay so long as there were only

one or two families, but when the congregation began to look too black, they kicked my dad out of there, too. (Letter)

At the end of his Bronx ministry Luigi Turco became increasingly involved in "the Movement of the New Thought; of churches based on the metaphysical interpretation of the Bible; of churches which were interested mainly in the healing of the minds and bodies of the people" ("Brief Story" 12–13). His reading of Troward, Eddy, and Holmes had prepared him for this involvement which he had "been looking for since" he "was converted in 1915" ("Brief Story" 13). These authors are often considered closely related to or part of the metaphysical and Protestant mix known as New Thought. This optimistic belief in mind power had its origins in the late nineteenth century and remains part of the contemporary American belief landscape. New Thought, Kate Bowler has written, "argued that people shared in God's power to create by means of thought. People shaped their own worlds by their thinking, just as God had created the world using thought. Positive thoughts yielded positive circumstances, and negative thoughts yielded negative situations" (14). During 1956 and 1957 Turco attended "lectures practically every day on Religious Science, on Theosophy, Psychology, Spiritualism, Astrology, Hinduism, etc." ("Brief Story" 14). He took courses with New Thought thinkers Dr. Paul Brunet and Dr. Ervin Seale. He did not receive the call to another Baptist Church and so, he said, it became "clear to me that the Spirit wants me to start a church, based on New Thought, here in Meriden [. . .]" ("Brief Story" 14). He preached in the ballroom of an old hotel to his son Gene (Lewis was then in the Navy) and three refugees whom he had assisted after the end of World War II. A fire destroyed the hotel and then Rev. Turco turned to writing. He died on September 18, 1968. As Lewis Turco wrote, "he was watching the evening news (his favorite show) when he pitched forward out of his chair and was gone" (Letter).

In the longest section of his spiritual autobiography, "The Wisdom of the Bible" composed as a letter to Pino—a nephew in Italy, Luigi Turco explained many of his New Thought beliefs. Neither of creeds nor dogmas, nor to be found in any particular church, the truth of the Bible, according to Turco, is "divine inspiration given to man through intuition" ("Wisdom" 22). Furthermore, "since the revelation of God to man is continuous, it is evident that man must be ready to change his mind when a new revelation comes to him" ("Wisdom" 29). Turco believed that one of the problems in the churches of 1960s America was that church leaders were not open to new spiritual discoveries.

> We do change our old ideas and substitute new ones in all realms of life. We have done so in agriculture, in certain sciences, in means of transportation, in education, in art, in industry, etc. Why should we not also do it in religion, since the old ideas of God for the salvation of mankind do not satisfy us and have not given us the redemption we all badly need? ("Wisdom" 34)

Soon after Rev. Turco returned from Riesi he deepened his encounter with New Thought and this awakened him. The Old World had not restored him in such a manner, but each event—leaving his church in Meriden, returning to Italy, briefly leading the Bronx church, and finding a new source of faith—had been part of God's plan. Yet the addressee of his text, Pino, resided in Italy, and so Rev. Turco had not completely abandoned the past or a contemporary Italian American identity. To receive God's blessings, Turco told Pino, "it is necessary that he see always the good in all adversities of life" ("Wisdom" 41). He used an analogy to clarify this notion: "In the realm of electrical science, the negative and the positive elements must join together to produce light or electric power. Thus the adversities are the means which God uses to lead man to complete his evolution to act positively in all unpleasant events of his existence to produce the good he wants" ("Wisdom" 41). Positive thoughts will have positive effects. "If our thoughts are thoughts of love, of forgiveness, of giving uplifting words to people with whom we come in contact in our daily living—thoughts of joy, of peace, or good will—we shall reap events of the same kind [. . .]" ("Wisdom" 62).

Some of this powerful positive thought begins to sound like a suburban-designed salvation. "We all have the desire to have good health; to have an adequate income to face the expenses of living a comfortable life without anxiety; to have peace of mind for ourselves and for our families; to live in harmony with our neighbors" and these desires, Turco says, are not only universal, but are ones that God wants us to fulfill ("Wisdom" 120). If this sounds like Gina and John Conning freed from their New Jersey split-level trap, then it is surely interesting that one of the examples provided to illustrate the possibility of positive lives comes from neither Paramus nor Wallingford, but from Riesi, Italy. Turco returned there once more in 1962, and "about three months before" leaving Connecticut, he heard that his niece Sarina "was engaged to one of her colleagues in the institution in Mazzarino [Sicily] where she taught school" ("Wisdom" 137). She had planned to marry once before but the relationship didn't work out (negative). The new relationship, Turco told Pino, was much better (positive). And so he told his Catholic priest nephew, "This news gave me much happiness because I proved to myself and to my brother the truth presented by the New Thought Movement about the teachings of Jesus, namely, that there is no evil in life, if we see only the good side of what appears to be evil to us" ("Wisdom" 137).

In sermons from the early 1960s, Turco names and praises the New Thought Movement and quotes from Erwin Seale and Thomas Troward. Turco offers words of hope to men in what sociologist David Riesman called "the lonely crowd." In "Your Silent Partner," preached two weeks before Easter, he advises "to find the enemy inside" and reasons, "Since God is the Creator of the World, then man is the creator of his world. The power of Creation is done through thinking, and man is furnished with this power of thinking" (1). Loneliness is one of the main forces, Turco says, that deter us from achieving our full potential. Loneliness leads to other concerns both physical and mental. Gina Conning, for example, suffered in the unfamiliar suburban environment, married to the ambitious son of a manufacturing company owner who seemed to compete with his dad to see who could work the longest hours. Turco would have told Gina what he told the small audience gathered in the ballroom of an old hotel. One is never alone. One ever has a companion and that "silent partner" is God. (This is similar to Miss Lindsay's words of comfort to Luigi in Ruddy's novel.) If one listens to the voice of God within, "the whispering of the Spirit of God" (4), then things will work out for the best. That voice can guide a person to his or her true path "which will help them to make a good living without struggle and tension" (3). Turco tells a biographical anecdote that makes it quite clear God is not just a silent life-partner, but a business one as well. Lou Austin, Turco says, "followed the voice" and his resort business "increases every year" and so "God for him is now His Senior Partner" (4). Each of us must become "a coworker with God" (5). In a sermon called "Man, Know Thyself" Turco quotes Matthew 21:22: "'All things, whatsoever ye shall ask in prayer, believing, ye shall receive.'"

It may be too simplistic to call the material aspirations delineated in Turco's sermons an embodiment of crass American suburban goals (what Kate Bowler and others call "the prosperity Gospel"). For example, in "The Redemption of the Body" Turco uses for his illustrations the Italian heroes Galileo and Columbus and an ordinary Italian woman from his former congregation in Meriden. In other words, Turco still keeps faith with things Italian as well as American. Turco notes near the end of this Kennedy-era sermon: "the terrific advancement in technology is scaring us because if another war will come the entire civilization will be destroyed. What we need [is a] terrific advance in the spiritual life" (7). Perhaps in order to advance we need to reconnect with the past. Galileo and Columbus listened to the God voice within, Turco says, but the contemporary Italian living in Connecticut did not.

∽

The Methodists of Portland, Maine built a Gothic Revival church in 1856, known on its completion as "the finest church edifice in all of New England" (Administrative Note 2). For a century the church flourished, adding additions to the building and fostering various branch churches, including two Italian churches. Then things began to change at mid-century. The Chestnut Street Church joined the National Register of Historic Places in 1977 and the congregations from the two Italian churches, and others, had been absorbed by the larger church. Though the Church prospered in the 1970s and '80s, perhaps its designation as a historic site predicted that it belonged to a prior age. At the end of the century membership and finances declined and at the start of the new century, in 2006, the historic church structure was decommissioned and sold. A new age had dawned. Portland had become a successful tourist destination. The Chestnut Street Church reopened as an upscale restaurant. As the Maine Historical Society describes its transformation:

> The exterior of the old church remains intact; the many stained glass windows on both sides and the front entry of the building remain untouched; the original pews serve as seating in the dining area; the old organ (case), although gutted prior to purchase, serves as a wait staff station, the original pulpit has become the hostess station, and the restaurant's kitchen is where the altar once stood. (Administrative Note 2)

One can read into this metamorphosis the commonplace that today in America mainline Protestant churches face difficult challenges as their utility bills increase in cost and their congregations decrease in size. Rev. Arthur Caliandro, son of Rev. Tommaso Calinadro—the minister for the Portland Italian Methodist Churches—became the successor to Rev. Norman Vincent Peale—the minister to America's oldest Protestant congregation, Marble Collegiate Church on Fifth Avenue in New York City. Rev. Arthur Caliandro challenged the commonplace notions regarding mainline Protestant churches at the end of the twentieth century. He initiated new ministries and he mastered a new speaking style. Yet, at the same time, he never forsook his ethnic heritage.

Arthur Calinadro embodied, put into practice the postethnic perspective that sociologist David A. Hollinger described in the mid-1990s. Hollinger said that such a perspective "favors voluntary over involuntary affiliations, balances an appreciation for communities of descent with a determination to make room for new communities, and promotes solidarities of wide scope that incorporate people with different ethnic and racial backgrounds" (3). That description works well to depict the goals and practices of Calinadro at Marble Collegiate, where he served as Senior Minister from 1984 to 2009. (He began there in 1967 as Minister of Evangelism. In 1975 he became an Associate Minister.) Caliandro both learned from and rebelled against aspects of his father's and his mentor's ministries. By doing so, by forming his own hybrid ministry, he succeeded in revitalizing a bastion of mainline Christianity without needing to forsake or alter his identity—indeed his affiliation, as Hollinger would have it—became strengthened by the effort.

In his memoir essay "A Methodist Boyhood," Arthur Caliandro provides the fullest depiction available of the origins of his life as a minister. Not only was Arthur the son of a minister, but he would grow up to be the brother of two other ministers, older brother Bruno and younger brother Ernest. As a young man Arthur moved easily from the Wesley of Methodism to the Calvin of the Reformed Church. While it is true that Norman Vincent Peale made the same fluid change, as we have seen, many Italian Protestant ministers moved with ease from denomination to denomination. Arthur may have received his strong sense of ecumenical spirit from his father who attempted to reach out to other faiths in Portland, including Catholics, not for purposes of proselytization but for mutual understanding, and felt discouraged when such efforts failed (205). Additionally, the Portland Italian Methodist Church served immigrants and therefore, as we have repeatedly seen, it had social-service concerns as well as spiritual ones. Arthur Caliandro took this whole-life approach out of the immigrant church and into an affluent mainline church. He forged programs of all sorts—some of which will be described briefly later. Marble Collegiate under his guidance was not simply or only a high-society church full of the power of positive thinking.

Calinadro begins his memoir as I began this book. He says, "It is natural to assume that all Italians are Catholics, but that is not so" (203). He then tells of his heritage, noting that his father—from Ciegli, near Bari—was born a Catholic. But his local priest alienated Tommaso, and at the root of their disagreement happened to be the Bible and Tommaso's desire to read and study it. Tommaso's three brothers also became Protestants. Arthur's mother, Francesca, however, came from Sicily and she was the only member of this Sicilian family to turn to Protestantism. Arthur notes, "her religious background was not very strong. There was no religion really [. . .]" (205). Once again we see repeated and shared occurrences: Bible reading, disagreement with a priest, and insincere religious affiliation. That these elements were repeated over and over again does not render these family narratives into folktales, but rather attests to their reality *for a small number of Italians*. By the way, it was the singing of hymns—another repeated aspect of conversion narratives—that first attracted Tommaso to Methodism. While walking with a friend in Rome, they heard singing coming from a Methodist church and entered (204).

After study at Drew Theological Seminary in Madison, New Jersey, Tommaso served the Italian Methodist Church in Portland from 1928 to 1950. Arthur says that "from the very beginning, my father leaned toward being more American than Italian" (206). Like so many other children of immigrants, Arthur says neither he and his brothers nor his parents emphasized learning, knowing Italian. Everyone wanted to be American.

Arthur also had the "isolation" (206) of being Italian Protestant in a community of 99 percent Italian Catholic. He felt other kinds of alienation growing up. He legally changed his birth name, Arturo, when an undergraduate at Ohio Wesleyan: "It was uncomfortable saying Arturo Caliandro in an Anglo-Saxon setting" (207). Also during college, he reveals in *Lost and Found* as well as in his autobiographical essay, he dated a young woman he liked very much, but she inexplicably and abruptly ended their relationship. He later found out that her parents forbid their dating because of his Italian heritage. "I remember thinking," Caliandro writes, "that they disliked me without even knowing me. That was very painful to me" (*Lost and Found* 164).

In a sermon he delivered late in his life titled "A Gift of Hard Times," he told the packed sanctuary of Marble Collegiate that "hard times often bear great gifts" (*Simple Faith*). Caliandro practiced what he preached, learned the lessons he espoused firsthand. In *Simple Steps* he proclaims:

> I have always been appalled, and still am shocked, by the dislikes, prejudices, and hatred people have for others because they're of a different religion, race, nationality, or sexual orientation. Because of any kind of difference.
>
> I am appalled I think because, when I was a child, I was aware that my parents had immigrated here from another country. We felt that one great thing about life in America was that many people, with many differences, had come together to make a great country. (107)

Caliandro adds that on some occasions he "got a sense of what it feels like to be disliked and cut off simply because of [his] heritage" (109). These are lessons he carried into his ministry, where he successfully became a community builder for diverse groups.

In *Make Your Life Count* Caliandro states that the two most influential people in his life were an English teacher and his father. From his father he received "a set of high moral standards" (49). Though he does not list Rev. Norman Vincent Peale here, perhaps he would have if he had listed the three or four most influential people in his life. Tommaso Caliandro brought the gospel to working-class immigrants and Norman Vincent Peale "to businessmen"—as Arthur Caliandro wrote, Peale "would share with them a practical Christianity that would help them with their everyday problems" (*Make Your Life Count* 10). Yet, Arthur Caliandro saw in Rev. Peale those same moral standards he saw in his own father. In his memoir-essay he says that "Dr. Peale stuck his neck out when he planned the succession" at Marble Collegiate (209). After all, Marble Collegiate may be the oldest Protestant Church in America, founded by the Dutch East India Company in 1628, but that heritage alone does not guarantee an existence marked by high moral standards. Marble Collegiate when Caliandro joined the staff (1967) also inescapably existed in an America of strife and possibility. Caliandro continues, "I had been here two years, he [Peale] put his hand on my shoulder and said, 'I want you to succeed me.' My being Italian seemed to make no difference to him" (209).

Caliandro, at Peale's request, began preaching at the early Sunday service while the elder minister continued with the later service. Peale, the great orator, preached to a packed sanctuary. Caliandro, the novice or so he saw himself, spoke to one or two hundred souls spread out across the large space. Caliandro recalls the three years he split Sunday preaching duties with Peale as the three most difficult years of his life. And yet, as he put it, "the hard times have the beautiful gifts" ("A Gift of Hard Times"). When Peale pushed the younger minister into the deep end of the ministerial pool the latter was forced to grow, forced to be self-reliant, and forced to learn how to preach ("A Gift of Hard Times"). The recordings—DVD, webcast, YouTube—of Caliandro show that he indeed did learn to preach. They also show a packed sanctuary. One story indicates that media initiatives also had an impact on his preaching. Marble Collegiate began a cable television program at the early date of 1975. Arthur's brother Bruno directed the television series. He told Arthur to get out from behind the lectern—movement away from it would make better television.

No doubt some of Arthur Caliandro's professors at Union Theological Seminary had an influence on his preaching style. For example, the use of three examples in a sermon was a well-learned seminary lesson. Another lesson he learned even at an earlier age. When his father took him to hear evangelists, young Arturo reacted negatively. Arthur recalled years later in a sermon, "The preacher worked on guilt and fear to get people to accept his beliefs [. . .]" ("Jesus Is Not the Problem" 2). On another occasion, when Arthur was a teenager, an evangelist warned, " 'If you people of Portland don't repent, if you don't change your ways, God is going to drop an atomic bomb in Portland Harbor' " ("Jesus Is Not the Problem" 2). Caliandro often spoke in his preaching of a judgmental Jesus and a loving Jesus. He was convinced and could convince others through his learned yet relaxed and casual preaching style that the true Jesus was the latter, the loving one.

Rev. Caliandro didn't do anything unusual or innovative in his preaching. What he did, he did well, but all of his skills were those of classical public speaking. For example, he never looked down at any text or notes but remained in constant eye contact with his audience (though sometimes he would pick up a sheet with a quotation from a favorite author and read it). He used hand gestures and strategic pauses. He used metaphors and lists; repetition for emphasis and reference to Biblical quotation and cultural texts. He referred to his own life and his own weaknesses and challenges. After an illness affected his voice, he effectively used a whisper in his preaching. Most of all he used narrative. Arthur Caliandro was a good storyteller.

In *Simple Steps* Caliandro tells a story about the time his father came to preach at Union Theological Seminary. At the time Arthur was in his final year and the faculty included world-famous theologian Reinhold Niebuhr. Tommaso Caliandro, according to his son, still "felt somewhat inferior because he had immigrated to this country, and he still spoke with a heavy Italian accent" (195), and so the day represented a very significant occasion for the elder Caliandro. In his sermon Tommaso spoke "about a man who had an experience with an angel" (195). After the sermon, Arthur, who at the time believed in the power of reason, asked his father why he spoke about men and angels. The son could see that he had upset his father. The lesson of this story seems to be do not place too much importance in the rational.

He tells another story in this book about reason and preaching style. Many years after seminary he attended a conference with twenty-six other clergy members, many of whom preached during a morning devotional. Arthur recalls that all gave "talks much like the ones we had all learned to write as sermons when we were in seminary" (132). Somewhat like Gilbert Tennent warning an "unconverted ministry," Caliandro bemoans, "no person shared anything of himself in those talks. There was no heart. No spirit" (132). Don't overestimate reason, but also don't discount passion. Caliandro, "with no well-defined goal in mind," decided "to share part of [his] own journey [. . .]" (132). And so he began, "'This morning my devotional will be a story of my own pain and brokenness and the healing that followed'" (132). He "held nothing back" and even referred to his psychiatrist. In other words, his testimony does not mirror that of an eighteenth-century American pastor's, such as Tennent, but perhaps Caliandro mixed some traditional American Protestant new light techniques with contemporary practices and with lessons learned from his Italian immigrant father as well as those learned in seminary and from life.

If personal parable-like stories became an important part of Rev. Caliandro's homiletic practice, Biblical and cultural reference also mattered. In *Simple Steps* he refers to scripture approximately fifteen times, and to authors or cultural figures—mostly contemporary—twenty-eight times. From scripture, he quotes Jesus or describes an action of Christ as illustration about eight times and also refers to Genesis, Psalms, Isaiah, and Paul. Among the authors quoted or cultural figures mentioned are Oliver Wendell Holmes, Jane Kenyon, Bernie Siegel, Goethe, Tennyson, Rilke, Thoreau, Mark Twain, Luciano Pavarotti, Pearl Bailey, and Bill Cosby. Many of the illustrations, quotations, and stories found here are also heard in his sermons. Of course, it is very likely they appeared first in sermon form and then were adapted for the book.

In *Lost and Found* Caliandro reveals that his ease before an audience was not easily achieved, but rather grew out of disciplined practice. He admits:

> The times that I feel the greatest freedom when speaking, when I feel most in control of myself and my material, are those times when I was best prepared. That preparation demands an enormous number of hours spent thinking, reading, and processing, not to mention the time I spend doubting myself, my material, and the words I will use to express my message. (ix)

Later in *Lost and Found*, along similar lines he points out: "it takes an enormous amount of time to prepare a sermon. I write a section. Then I write it again. Then again. Often, I go back to the beginning and rethink my fundamental concept" (76).

His expressed attitude in these sermons often communicated a kind of New Thought theology. Here is where Luigi Turco, Norman Vincent Peale, and Arthur Caliandro meet. Like Turco, Caliandro spoke often of the "God-spark." Like Peale, Caliandro incorporated catchy upbeat phrases into sermons and his writings. "The best place to start," Caliandro said in *Simple Steps*, "is wherever you are today" (34). Bowler described Peale's preaching as "cheery and anecdotal" (55). Peale, she said, "taught that any person could access God's power through positive thinking, which directed spiritual energy toward the attainment of health, self-esteem, or business acumen" (57). As Luigi Turco said,

God wants us to be happy: "God, our Father, wants his children to live happy, harmonious lives, so he will lead us to do the very thing or the very kind of work which will give us the income and the character needed to live joyful lives [. . .]" ("Wisdom of the Bible" 120). And Caliandro wrote, "When we [. . .] become disciplined in our religious practice, we can achieve more in the real world. Whatever your faith may be, forge a deeper alliance with it and you will be surprised to see how it will increase your effectiveness and level of achievement in the real world" (*Lost and Found* 78). And in a sermon from his final year as Senior Minister at Marble Collegiate, Caliandro preached, "On your job, going to work tomorrow, if you have a bad attitude, remember you have the power to choose. Change your attitude" ("Always Walk Towards the Light" 4).

He preached his final sermon before retirement on February 1, 2009. In "Go with Faith," one of the very first things he says is that he is an Italian. He uses anecdote and humor (lots of humor) and some repetition in this sermon about "finding ways to love one another." He speaks with encouraging optimism. "The best in life is all about finding ways to love one another," he says. "Everything we have is in the moment," he says. "The best we can do is strive to love," he says. He tells a story about how by boat he chased the beautiful golden reflection of the sun on the surface of the bay near his Maine vacation home. He came to realize that he had been "surrounded by gold and didn't even know it." From a revelation of his own weakness, his own human frailty he gladly reassures the congregation: "You and I are in the gold."

Rev. Caliandro welcomed all to share in that "gold." Like Rev. Turco had in the Bronx, Caliandro reached out to others from his Fifth Avenue Manhattan church. Caliandro established programs for understanding across faiths; educational opportunities for low-income children; appointed women to the church's board; led an effort to build a church in Budapest, Hungry after the end of Soviet domination; and established a meeting place at the church for gay and lesbian members. The latter effort in the mid-1990s resulted in a protest and in some congregants leaving the church. Caliandro persevered, however, and continued to act as a builder of community in the city. Some of his initiatives may be like social service work, and in this sense analogous to the ethnic mission churches of the early twentieth century. But Marble Collegiate's efforts under Caliandro's leadership at the close of the twentieth century and following were "beyond multiculturalism."

In his memoir essay of 1987—and so twenty-five years of his life he still had in front of him—he said of Marble Collegiate:

> In terms of my relationship with the church, I don't worry about being Italian anymore, though at the beginning I wondered, because it was so different from my background and so Anglo-Saxon. It has become a church where there is an enormous mix of peoples, even though there are very few Italians. The national groups, the religious backgrounds of the people, are so varied that I feel very normal and natural. And it surprises and pleases me that my not being a WASP does not make any difference to some of the old families of New York who are members. (209)

I have said that I do not like to make large generalizations, but nonetheless I have made some. Among them are ones that perhaps seem contradictory. For example, I have said that Italian Protestants were radicals of a sort who confronted alienation in Italy and America. In America one of the ways to negotiate old and new world ways was through Protestantism. Yet, this very Protestantism could become a conservative move, a nonconformity followed by a redefined conformity: but perhaps never completely so, never simply so. Rev. Arthur Calinadro may have had his summer home in Maine—symbol of his middle-class mainstream comfort—but he also maintained his Italian identity and his ability to challenge the complacent.

All identity positions are ever in-flux and inherently slippery and continually open to personal and social transformations and refigurations. In Southern Italy the embrace of Protestantism can be interpreted as a socially emancipatory and antiestablishment move. But in America the position could become inverted. When large numbers of immigrants arrived in the United States it was avowedly a "Protestant" nation. When Italians embraced Protestantism in the United States, it functioned to temper their old identity and contributed to a new one, Italian American. This transformation in identity underlines the complexity of all such positions.

We have seen that Rev. Mangano could be a booster for United States imperialism, but bemoaned American consumerism. We have seen that my great-grandfather maintained such a strong Italian identity that he never became a US citizen, and this attitude may have posed problems for him with the American Baptist church. We have seen at the same time that Rev. Turco's congregation sought a less ethnic pastor, he embraced a twentieth-century version of Emersonian self-reliance. We have seen that Rev. Caliandro flourished in one of the nation's landmark churches, but also that he challenged the status-quo of Fifth Avenue society. When he delivered his retirement sermon he made a point to identify himself as "Italian," an "Italian" who no doubt differed from Mangano's "Italian." Mangano may have always pushed for Americanization, but his Americanization differed from Rev. Ives's. For Ives, Americanization may have meant or promised conformity in a land of steady habits, but for Mangano it meant great change for the immigrant. The hopeful work of helping immigrants negotiate the demands of two worlds remains a challenge for both America and Italy.

Epilogue

> Finding unfamiliar the familiar context in which a person is born is the experience of many people who have chosen another place to live. It does not mean that the new location is an ideal place. The new location is only outside one's past.
>
> —Graziella Parati, *Migration Italy*

Italians converted to or expressing some interest in Protestantism often left Italy for work in America—and American, English, and Italian missionaries would cite such departures as one of the difficulties that they had to confront. In America, similarly, Italian immigrants would leave one city or town for another in search of a job. In 1905 the Italian Baptist Mission in New Haven reported that "many [members] have left the city to secure work elsewhere [. . .]" (Chivers 194). Chas. Edward Prior, president of the Hartford Baptist Union, reported in this same year that "one of the discouraging features of this work is the fact that Italians are frequently obliged to go from place to place in search of work, so that many of those who have been converted and joined the church here have left us for other fields" (Chivers 196).

In addition to geographic movement, missionaries in America confronted obstacles of all sorts rooted in fear and prejudice just as they had in Italy. Vincenzo di Domenica noted in 1902 that when preaching outdoors in Haverhill, Massachusetts, "a gang of Italian drunken men interrupted" and succeeded in breaking "up our hopeful services." Di Domenica asked the City Marshall for help, "but," di Domenica wrote, "as he is an Irish Catholic man, strongly objected to my request [. . .]" (231).

Vincenzo's brother recorded on the same page of the *Baptist Home Mission Monthly* that in Newark, New Jersey, open-air meetings had been successful with as many as "four or five hundred hearers [. . .]," but, di Domenica adds, "the work is very hard for me [. . .]" with each Sunday "two Sunday Schools to attend and three preaching services, besides an open-air meeting" ("Interesting Italian Work" 231). Although exhausted by the end of the day, he loved, he said, preaching the Gospel and would "make any sacrifice whatsoever" to do so (231).

Not all Italian Americans are Catholic. The Italian American experience is much richer and more diverse than usually believed to be. The preceding pages have examined the complex history of the lived experience of people who engaged in an alternative religious practice in their homeland and then navigated traditional and dominant ways in their adopted land. Each immigrant's story has its uniqueness; a person is not a peg drilled to fit a pattern.

Could it be because of a hint of scandal that the Baptist Church and Rev. Barone parted ways rather than due to "lack of funds" as suggested by Melchisedec Barone ("Obituary"), and could the year have been 1913 instead of 1910? A brief, though front-page, story in the *Bridgeport Evening Farmer*, April 24, 1913, reported that an ill infant in South Norwalk died after having been visited by "'Rev. Dr. Alfred Barone.'" The South Norwalk mission had been established by Vincenzo di Domenica in 1903. *The Baptist Home Mission* noted in 1905, "There are 400 Italians in the city, and they have cut loose from Romanism, are superstitious and ignorant, and do not profess any kind of religion at all" (Chivers 197). When Barone followed di Domenica at Stamford, he continued to serve this satellite mission. The newspaper story notes that the medical examiner requested the coroner also look into the matter. Rev. Barone, the story continued, answered the child's "Italian-speaking" mother's request for assistance, but as a chiropractor Barone may not have been able to aid in an instance of pneumonia. The mother "was under the belief that she had called a regular physician" ("Chiropractor's Case Reported"). According to Rev. Mangano, "It is one of the axioms of Christian work that the personal life of the worker is far more potent in the long run than what he or she may say" (*Sons of Italy* 182). Perhaps Rev. Barone's work as a chiropractor transgressed in this instance his "Christian work." The coroner reported:

> Barone was not a licensed practitioner in this state, and was not a member of any of the recognised, as regular schools

of medicine, but was a member of the Chiropractic School, having graduated September 1912 from and through the written correspondence method of teaching affected by the socalled [sic] "National Chiropractic School" of Chicago, Illinois. ("Coroner's Report" 365)

Certainly from a present-day perspective Barone misdiagnosed the patient, and he should have referred the mother to an appropriate physician. As John J. Phelan, the coroner, put it, the child "might have been saved under the treatment by a reasonably well educated licensed physician of this state" (366). However, he concluded, "I should be loth [sic] to ascribe criminal omission or negligence to him [Barone] in causing the death of the child" (366).

Rosina Barone, mother of Alfredo and Giovanni, stayed at home in Italy, but seems to have desired to visit her sons in America, or to move there permanently. From a series of postcards (*cartoline*) sent to Alfredo during the early twentieth century it is apparent that Rosina lived in difficult conditions and felt abandoned by her sons.

Alfredo was born on May 25, 1869 to Rosina Salzano, age twenty-eight, who had been born in Caserta, and at the time lived in Salerno, and Guglielmo Barone, age forty-two, a clerk (*impiegato*) born in Foggia and also at the time lived in Salerno. Guglielmo and Rosina were married in Foggia on October 26, 1871. Alfredo, therefore, was born out of civil wedlock, though it is possible that Guglielmo and Rosina were married in a church ceremony previously ("Estratto"). According to my grandfather's typed obituary for Alfredo, when young Alfredo turned away from the Catholic Church and converted to Protestantism, "he was disowned by his aristocratic parents." Younger brother Giovanni was born in 1877, went to America in 1898, where he first worked in a Mount Vernon, New York piano factory but then answered a call in 1904 to serve as pastor to the Italian Baptist Church in Waterbury, Connecticut, from which he retired in 1917. He died in 1938.

From Foggia in May of 1905 Rosina wrote her eldest:

> I received your note. I thank you with my heart and bless the good you have done. I am very distressed about the illness of your wife and I send great courage, even from me. Giovanni sent me 20 lira with which I was able to celebrate a blessed and Happy Easter. I sent you a newspaper in which you'll read of the events in Foggia. I wish to come visit you

but I can't since I am living so far away from you in this way. With hugs and blessings, Your Mother

What did she mean by those two ambiguous phrases "even from me" and "in this way"? Although Rosina wrote in a very formal and for the most part clear handwriting and in nondialect Italian, some of her comments are difficult to understand without sufficient context, and yet provide a reader with the sense of conflict between mother and eldest son.

Did having *two* Protestant sons, even if thousands of miles away, make it difficult for Rosina to get the necessary papers for journeying outside the country? Did the triangle of residence—Caserta, Salerno, and Foggia—add to such difficulty? In June of 1906 she wrote from Foggia:

> I'm writing to you with much displeasure because I haven't heard anything from you or your brother. I go to the post office everyday and find nothing. Tell me, do you want me to ask the Signorina for food? May God bless you all for all you have done to me. Giovanni wrote to me about a month and a half ago [. . .] but there was no money. Dear, I'm writing to your brother as well. I am down and without money. What should I do? Should I leave myself in the middle of the street? You could have written [. . .] With love, without money, your mother

Clearly, Rosina chided Alfredo here and did so with biting sarcasm: "bless you," she told her minister son, "for all you have done to me"; not *for* me.

Two years later she reported that she had finally secured the necessary documents for travel, but remained short of the needed cash. She said she would soon leave for Naples and then would "die with you" in America. She closed, "write a letter because I haven't seen one," but also added, "all the best and kisses to the babies."

The following year she still hadn't left and still pleaded with her son to write each time she wrote to him. She had someone named Biagio Comci assisting her, and he wrote to the police, the consulate, and others on her behalf. It is not clear what specific difficulties she faced. "It's useless to tell you," she wrote, "the state of misery and the shame of our family and how we live." Once again she ended with a plea: "try to send me soon some assistance if you don't really want to disappoint me." It is unknown to me why Alfredo seemed to be indifferent to the needs of his mother and how this troubling drama concluded.

Alfredo married Rosina Santoro in Bari, Italy on June 11, 1894. (Their first son, Melchisedec, had been born in Foggia on July 1, 1893.) They spent their lives together, Alfredo predeceasing his wife by six years. A minister's wife not only ran the household but assisted in the ministry. Oftentimes minister's wives taught Sunday school. Alfredo founded his Alpha Omega Assembly on October 1, 1910, while in the middle of his three years as pastor of the Stamford Italian Baptist Church. Years later when he had placards made promoting the Assembly, both Rose and Alfredo were pictured in a matched set, both radiated intelligence more than pastoral kindness in their expressions, and below both images is a brief prayer made partly of Psalm 115:14; but an appeal for funds (and a somewhat indirect one at that) appears only beneath Alfredo's (here it's "Alfred") image. In a 1916 Alpha and Omega newsletter article titled "Il Matrimonio," Rev. Barone wrote: "Il matrimonio è sublime [. . .]," and "Il matrimonio non è l'unione accidentale e passeggiera per la semplice riproduzione della specie, come lo è per gli animale, ma, esso è l'unione indissolubile e perpetua di tutta la vita" ("Marriage is sublime [. . .]," and "Marriage is not an accidental union and journey simply for the reproduction of the species, like it is for animals, but it is an indissoluble union and lasts for all of life") (April 1, 1916, 4). Somehow one of these matched sets of images reached the Baptist Union of Italy Archive in Torre Pellice. I have an accomplished oil portrait of Rev. Barone, which according to the attached shipping label came from the Orfanotrofio Evangelico Battista e Casa di Riposa (Baptist Orphanage and Rest Home) via Delle Spighe 8 Centocelle Roma, and reached my grandfather in Brooklyn during the summer of 1956. Alfredo and Rose did not become naturalized United States citizens. They worked together, raised a large family together, and lived in a space between America and Italy.

Some of the Italian American Protestant ministers married Anglo American wives. Antonio Mangano married Mabel Austin Farnham, a graduate of Vassar College. Pietro Sbrocco, older brother of the singer and musician Vincenzo, ministered to the Italian Baptists of Bristol, Connecticut, "with," the *Baptist Home Mission Monthly* reported, "the efficient help of his newly wedded American wife with whom he became acquainted through her service among the Italian missions under the Women's Board" (Bruce 477). Rev. Luigi Turco, a Baptist minister, as well, also met his wife, May Putnam, through her missionary work with Italian immigrants. Mom May, as son poet Lewis Turco refers to her, could trace her lineage to John Putnam, who settled in Salem, Massachusetts in 1639 or 1640.

In Italy today women have a very prominent role in the Protestant churches. The Unione Cristiana Evangelica Battista d'Italia, founded in 1956, has had and currently has many women pastors and many women in prominent executive positions. Rev. Anna Maffei, for example, recently led the organization. During the 150 Years of Baptist Witness in Italy conference, October 2013, Silvia Rapisarda, a minister, very kindly (and quietly) translated for me Martin Ibarra's interesting presentation, "Le chiese battiste dal periodo fascista alla crisi del 1968" ("The Baptist Church from the Fascist Period to the Crisis of 1968") just at the moment—after speaking, after lunch, after trying hard to follow various talks in Italian—that I grew weary. Her kindness I appreciated, but her facility at instantly (and very quietly) changing Ibarra's Italian into English quite amazed me. In a *breve ritratto* (brief portrait) that I read about Pastor Rapisarda, I learned of her commitment to working with the dispossessed, her reputation for acute intelligence, and her faith. She recalls as a teenager being asked, "Ma non hai paura che Dio non esista?" ("But aren't you afraid that God doesn't exist?") And she replied to her friend, "No, ho paura di scopire un giorno di non avere capito nulla di Dio, di avere frainteso tutto" ("No, I am afraid that I will discover one day that I have not caught a thing about God, that I have misunderstood everything") (Bouchard 20). Pastor Rapisarda has worked with Italy's poor and in its poorest regions. She now does several tasks in Rome, including serving as pastor for the Chapel at the Casa di Riposa (where once a portrait of Rev. Barone must have hung).

The Baptist as well as Lutheran, Methodist, and Waldensian Churches formed the Federazione delle Chiese Evangeliche in Italia in 1967, and this Federation of Protestant Churches in Italy supports women in leadership roles, the autonomy of member churches, missionary activities, a priesthood of all believers, local congregations as primary, religious freedom and separation of church and state (which is vastly more problematic in Italy than in the United States), emphasis on the direct reading and interpretation of Scripture, and aid to refugees and immigrants. Two subgroups of the Federation are the Federation of Protestant Women in Italy, founded in 1976, and the Department of Migrants and Refugees, founded in 1984. The latter advocates for the human rights of immigrants and asylum-seekers, and it aids immigrants' entrance into Italian society through a variety of programs similar to those offered by Protestant missions in the United States at the start of the previous century: help finding work, language classes, home economic classes for women, and so on (Federazione della Chiese Evangeliche website). The hostility toward immigrants from various nativist groups in Italy today also recalls similar anti-immigrant campaigns in the United States a century ago.

How do churches in Italy affect today's immigrants? How does Catholic centrality impact the assistance provided to immigrants by Protestant churches and organizations, and the transition of immigrants into contemporary Italian culture? Laura E. Ruberto has written in a study about contemporary Italy and similarities between women's emigration and immigration that "citizenship rights become tied to cultural appropriation" (79). Then must a contemporary migrant embrace Catholicism to appropriate an Italian identity?

Annalisa Frisina has recently written that "despite the significant secularization of Italian society [. . .], and despite considerable changes in the history of relations between Church and state [. . .], the Catholic Church has retained its dominant role in the public sphere" (272). This is especially true for religious education in Italian schools (something opposed by Italian Protestants). These classes are controlled by the Catholic Church, but are now offered to many children from non-Catholic migrant families. If Catholicism offered for many decades Italy's only means to construct a national identity as Enzo Pace (Frisina's teacher and mentor) has argued, then in contemporary Italy with its diversity of immigrant (and religious) voices has this "affiliation by *tradition*," as Pace has also argued, become "increasingly obsolete" (87)? Pace makes three important points regarding such national identity formation. He optimistically believes many different religious voices are "increasingly visible in the public sphere, adding color and identity to the symphony of voices attempting to speak publicly in religious terms" (88). He states that "the unanimous Catholicism of Italians conceals [. . .] a plurality of ways of conceiving the meaning of belonging to the Catholic Church" (88).Furthermore, he observes, the "daughters and sons of the first immigrants searching for a precarious equilibrium between their birth identity [Muslim] and their feeling of affiliation with the Italian national community" (94).

Carmelo Di Sano writing for *La Sentinella Italo-Americana* in 1925, a monthly magazine published by the Italian Priest's Fellowship of the Episcopal Church in America, noted that "After fifty years of great achievements we still find the nation of Italy, fighting those monsters of the past, illiteracy, ignorance and superstition" (3). Count Cavour might have famously proclaimed "*Libera chiesa in libero stato*" and after unification religious toleration might have expanded, but then in 1929 Mussolini's accords with the Vatican recognized Catholicism as the state religion and Protestants faced renewed persecution during the Fascist era. The 1948 constitution changed the Fascist mandate in theory but not in fact, and so, as stated previously, separate non-Catholic faiths have worked for legal recognition in contemporary Italy. Contemporary Italian journalist Pino Aprile does not paint the reunification of Italy as a "Risorgimento," as a rebirth of any kind or even as an improvement over what existed prior to it and he adds, "The worst may still be to come" (124). Frisina concludes that "the current Italian government and the Catholic powers [. . .] are determined to preserve the Concordat [the 1929 agreement] regime and the privileges it awards to the Catholic Church, starting from Catholic education in state schools," and that "the part of Italian society that is trying to make Italy become a country where there is more space for pluralism does not seem to have any political representation today" (280). Yet, she nonetheless believes, "In daily life, on the other hand, young people are already experiencing the growing religious diversity of Italian society" (280).

But what will this younger generation experience, and what choices will they make in the context of that experience? In a review of the documentary film about immigrants' right to citizenship in Italy, *18 Ius soli*, Nadine Wassef describes a sequence in which "Aziz, of Moroccan origin, speaks about his marriage to a Neapolitan woman as a deliberate attempt to integrate into an Italian community" (84). Aziz buys bread and eats pasta with his wife as he explains "that he purposely decided 'to marry someone who was not from Morocco but a girl from Naples'" (84).

In a brief memoir-essay, the great Italian American architect Robert Venturi, like Aziz, a son of immigrants, recalls that his parents "were born Catholics but did not practice" (197), and when he was five his parents became members of the Society of Friends (Quakers, and recall that one of the nicknames for Philadelphia is the Quaker City). Venturi says his father "without disowning his roots [. . .] felt that one did everything one could to become typically American" (198).

Mauro and Giovanna Toglia came to New Rochelle, New York from Calitri, Italy in the early years of the twentieth century. They became Protestants in New York, according to Maura Mandrano—their granddaughter—because of "the way the Irish priests and nuns treated the Italian immigrants" (e-mail correspondence with Barone, February 11–13, 2014). The local Italian Protestant Church, the Church of the Good Shepherd, provided services in Italian, but, in the words of Maura Mandrano: "When the small population could not sustain the little church anymore, they merged into the First Presbyterian Church of New Rochelle." Mandrano was not only baptized in this larger church, but also served as a deacon and sang in the choir. Despite the fact of her meaningful participation in the First Church, she told me: "I don't believe the First Presbyterian Church acknowledged the history of the Church of the Good Shepherd, at least not later during my lifetime (1955–). Had my mother and aunts not mentioned it to me I would never have known [. . .]."

All but forgotten are the Italian American Protestants.

She also told me that as a child she "most definitely was ostracized [. . .] by the parents of [her] Italian-American, Catholic playmates." Since she attended public schools rather than parochial ones, she established close ties with the Jewish community of New Rochelle, and since she became so active in the Presbyterian Church, she noted that "the strong Anglo-Saxon pull of that denomination made me closer to England than to Italy in my early life." She added that her family did not speak Italian at home, and in college she majored in English literature. But, she concluded, "I've since made up for it, though, by taking Italian classes, being active in our [Calitrani] group both online and off—and I WILL get to Calitri one of these days, I swear" (e-mail correspondence with Barone, February 11–13, 2014).

Another sort of return might be to an ancestor's faith rather than to a specific geographical place. Recently in the *New York Times* Benedicta Cipolla published an op-ed essay about her father, a Catholic priest. She noted that "despite his 100 percent Italian background, my dad grew up Methodist in Providence, R.I., in a family with anti-Catholic leanings" (September 20, 2015, SR8). Perhaps the sentence just quoted reveals Cipolla's assumption that all Italians are by nature Catholic, even though she knows firsthand that this is not so. Her father, she noted, "explored different churches" and found the Episcopal Church welcoming. He appreciated the ritual, and when his grandmother accompanied him to services "she was reminded of the Catholic chapel she had worshipped in as a child." Richard Gennaro Cipolla became an Episcopal priest, "but," his daughter stated, "Catholicism always pulled at him." In 1980 it became possible for married Episcopal priests to become Catholic priests, and Cipolla "was one of the first priests ordained under this process in the United States" (SR8). According to Benedicta Cipolla, there are "about 100 Catholic priests who are married, and used to be Episcopal priests" (SR8). That number is admittedly small, yet it nonetheless tells us something large, so Benedicta Cipolla argued and I would concur. Cipolla asserted that "tradition can evolve" (SR8), and that these married men are now priests indicates, she said, some evolution in the Church's thinking regarding married priests.

 I have been reluctant, to some extent, to say in this study what large statement these many small things observed and described can support. If the scholar may err by either completing a broad work that lacks significance because of weak evidence and hasty generalization or may have exhaustive particular research but fail to establish generalizations, I would say my folly might be the latter. In an essay published nearly thirty-five years ago in *Boundary 2*, I criticized the grand science-like impulse of Jonathan Culler's *Structuralist Poetics* and suggested instead "hundreds of ethnographies of poetics" ("Under the Silence" 130). "Ultimately," I wrote, "formulating rules of particular systems of convention will be more valuable for the study of cultures than for the search for the nebulous System" (131–132). And so even at an early stage in my thinking I advocated for particulars over generalities and plurality over singularity. I argued for humility over the hubris (as I saw it and still see it) of the "definitive."

 A single set of characteristics or a life narrative writ in an arrow-like flight cannot explain a culture. Nonetheless, generalizations have been made in these pages such as that Italian American Protestantism has been infrequently studied; that in Italy Protestantism had an oppositional quality to it, whereas in America it can be seen as a move toward the mainsteam and yet those who so moved also eagerly retained aspects of their Italian identity; that Protestant missionaries in Italy and America offered the enticement of literacy; that in Italy Protestants faced persecution and were condemned by some for being irreligious and by others for being too religious; that Protestantism in America offered some immigrants a means to figure out old world and new world ways more than it resulted in a double alienation of rejection by Catholic immigrants and condescension by Anglo Protestants; that the ministries of Rev. Barone and the history of the Italian Congregational Church of Hartford well illustrate the life cycle of an immigrant church; and that even as mainline Italian Protestant churches began to fade, ministers such as Turco and Caliandro still self-identified as Italian and held that identity dear.

Beyond Memory will be a catalyst for future work. If it raises questions rather than definitively answers them, well good: so be it. This brief book can be considered *l'antipasto* at the table for the study of Italian Protestants in Italy and America. Yes, *il primo piatto* and *il secondo piatto* may follow with a rich menu of choices for further study. For example, herein for the most part my sources have been Baptist, Congregational, Episcopal, Methodist, and Presbyterian, but the Assemblies of God Pentecostal denomination has had many Italian followers in Italy and in many of the diaspora nations. An Italian Pentecostal revival took place in Chicago in 1907. The sources that I have used demonstrate how much more might be gleamed from the tens of thousands of pages in denominational publications, such as those published by foreign and home missionary societies. I say little about lay leaders in these churches and only hint at the possibilities of an analysis of architecture and the material culture within churches. Not only do I discuss mostly mainline Protestant churches, but I have spoken almost completely about ministers—to some extent, even when I use literary sources such as novels. Open the churches up and look inside and who would be found sitting in the pews? What would demographic analyses reveal? And what of regional variation? Did a California Italian immigrant church differ from a Connecticut one, and what do the differences reveal about Italian Americans? In all future explorations of this field, a global perspective that keeps both Italy and America in mind will be a necessity. How could it be otherwise for Italian American studies?

Or for American studies? John Demos's recent book *The Heathen School*, a work about a nearly forgotten effort in nineteenth-century

Connecticut to evangelize young men from non-Christian societies and then send them home to "redeem" their native lands, is, he says, "'local,' yes, but it's also a national story, even an international one" (4). The Monson Baptist Church may have been small and local, but its congregants had been swept up in the movements of national economics and global migrations. Demos's book begins, like this one, in the personal as well: "My father," he says, "born of Greek parentage and raised in Istanbul, was educated just after the start of the last century at a place called Anatolia College, a missionary school in central Turkey. Indeed, the college's original sponsor was the very same American Board of Commissioners for Foreign Missions that played a key role in the story of the heathen school" of Cornwall, Connecticut, and the subject of Demos's study (6). Though his work begins in the local and the personal, it crosses into the national and global through thoughts about America as a redeemer nation, the nature of failure and success in America, and the boundaries between the marginal and mainstream in America. While working on his Connecticut story, Demos received a fund-raising brochure from Anatolia College, now located in northern Greece, and Demos looked closely at a picture in it: "And there, looking out at me from the middle of the photograph, is my father (age about eighteen), yet another heathen youth marked for salvation" (4).

This anecdote from the start of Demos's book reminds me of the time I went to see Alfredo and Rosina's grave at Woodland Cemetery in Stamford, Connecticut. I wanted to see this funerary monument because a photocopy of a photograph I had seen of it piqued my curiosity. It is a large stone and on top of it there is another smaller stone in the shape of an open book. What message, I wondered, did Rev. Alfredo have Joseph Cuva carve into this book? What message did my great-grandfather bequeath to all subsequent generations? What wise words did Rev. Alfredo Barone choose to leave and to share *in perpetuity*?

As I approached the large stone I could see the large letters that spelled simply: BARONE. (Alfredo's brother's monument at Pine Grove Cemetery in Waterbury is in the shape of a small stone bench with BARONE cut into it.) As I approached I could see the open book on top of the huge granite base. I paused and breathed deeply for a moment. What is the message, I wondered? What is the truth? I anticipated discovery, revelation, and prophecy.

And what is cut into the open book—nothing. It is blank, an empty page. The book is blank, I conjectured, because we must inscribe it with the story that is our own lives. The impetus to study the past often comes out of something familial, personal—as in Demos's example and as in mine (Greek—*historein*, to inquire). This is my open book and though its pages are full and it is finished, it may not yet be complete. Though I have traveled beyond my memory of family ancestors and into the larger world of national and global facts, and I have provided some interpretation of what these facts signify, the Barone story, the Italian American story, the American story, the human story calls for more stories, more evocations of cultural memory, of how the particular of any person or any ethnicity fits, resists, or alters that even-woven cloth of the nation and the world.

Works Cited

Abbate, William. E-mail correspondence to Dennis Barone. June 12–14, 2009; and conversation with Dennis Barone, September 16, 2013.
Abel, Theodore. *Protestant Home Missions to Catholic Immigrants*. New York: Institute of Social and Religious Research, 1933.
Anderson, J. S. *Heroes of the Faith in Modern Italy*. Glasgow: Pickering & Inglis, 1914.
"Angell Flays Radical Departures, Advising Return to Conservatism." *Yale News* October 12, 1935, 1.
Annual Report of the American Union Church Florence, Italy for 1868. Florence: Claudian Press, 1869.
Annual Report of the American Union Church Florence, Italy for 1869. Florence: Claudian Press, 1870.
Annual Report of the Committee of the Baptist Missionary Society. London: Alexander and Shepherd, 1890–1900. American Baptist Historical Society, Atlanta, Georgia.
Aprile, Pino. *Terroni: All That Has Been Done to Ensure that the Italians of the South Become "Southerns."* Translated by Ilaria Maria Rosiglioni. New York: Bordighera Press, 2011.
Arrighi, Antonio. *The Story of Antonio, the Galley-Slave*. New York: Revell, 1911.
Auster, Paul. *The Invention of Solitude*. New York: Penguin, 1988.
Barolini, Helen. *Umbertina*. 1979. New York: Feminist Press, 1999.
Barone, Alfredo. *Alpha and Omega Assembly* 1 (April 1916) [newsletter]. Yale Divinity School Library, Yale University, New Haven, CT.
———. "The Requirements necessary for the ministry's candidate examination." Manuscript. Yale Divinity School Library, Yale University, New Haven, CT.
———. *La vita di Gesù Cristo ossia l'armonia degli evangeli*. Bari: S. Angelo dei Lombardi, 1895.

Barone, Dennis. Interview with Rev. William Zito. June 17, 2009. Portland, CT.
———. "Under the Silence of the Unfinished Work." *Boundary 2* 10.2 (1982): 115–134.
Barone, Melchisedec. Obituary for Alfredo Barone. Typescript. July 29, 1950. Collection of the author.
Barone, Rosina. Correspondence to Alfredo Barone, 1905–1912. Collection of Denise and Pasquale DiFulco.
Bebbington, D. W. "The Early Developments of the Baptist Movement." *150 anni di presenza battista in Italia (1863-2013)*. Edited by Stefano Gagliano. Milan: Biblion edizioni, 2015, 9–27.
Belotti, Elena Gianini. *The Bitter Taste of Strangers' Bread: An Italian Immigrant in America*. Translated by Martha King. New York: Bordighera Press, 2012.
Bemportato, Domenico and Marco Davite, dirs. *Like the Salt of the Earth: 150 Years of Baptist Witness in Italy* (DVD). Rome: Unione Cristiana Evangelica Battista d'Italia, 2011.
Bencivenni, Marcella. *Italian Immigrant Radical Culture: The Idealism of the Sovversivi in the United States, 1890-1940*. New York: NYU Press, 2011.
Biller, Peter. "Goodbye to Waldensianism?" *Past and Present* 192 (2006): 3–33.
"Bloomfield." *Hartford Courant* March 7, 1904, 12.
Bouchard, Piera Egidi. "Quel Gesù amico: Silvia Rapisarda." *Il Seminatore* 102.2/3 (2013): 20–21.
Bowler, Kate. *Blessed: A History of the American Prosperity Gospel*. New York: Oxford University Press, 2013.
"Bristol Italians Organize Society." *Hartford Courant* January 20, 1911, 15.
Brodhead, Richard. "Strangers on a Train: The Double Dream of Italy in the American Gilded Age." *Modernism/Modernity* 1.2 (1994): 1–19.
Bruce, James M. "The Hartford Italian Mission." *Baptist Home Mission Monthly* 30 (December 1908): 474–477.
Burt, William. *Europe and Methodism*. Cincinnati: Jennings and Graham, 1909.
Caliandro, Arthur. "Always Walk Towards the Light." Marble Collegiate Church. http://www.marblechurch.org/SermonArchive/MonthlySermonBooklets/2009Library/January (accessed January 9, 2013).
———. "A Gift of Hard Times." *Simple Faith*, vol. 8. DVD. New York: Marble Collegiate Church, 2008.
———. "Go with Faith." Sermon preached February 1, 2009. Audio file. Marble Collegiate Church. www.marblechurch.org.
———. "Jesus Is Not the Problem." http://www.marblechurch.org/Sermons/2004Library/March2004/tabid/140/Default.aspx (accessed January 9, 2013).
———, with Barry Lenson. *Lost and Found: 23 Things You Can Do to Find Personal Freedom*. New York: McGraw-Hill, 2004.
———. *Make Your Life Count*. San Francisco: Harper & Row, 1990.

———. "A Methodist Boyhood." *Growing Up Italian*. Edited by Linda Brandi Cateura. New York: Morrow, 1987, 202–211.

———, with Barry Lenson. *Simple Steps: Ten Things You Can Do to Create an Exceptional Life*. New York: McGraw-Hill, 2000.

Calitri, Charles. *Father*. New York: Crown, 1962.

Cannistraro, Philip V. and Gerald Meyer. "Introduction Italian American Radicalism: An Interpretive History." *The Lost World of Italian-American Radicalism*. Edited by Philip V. Cannistraro and Gerald Meyer. Westport, CT: Praeger, 2003, 1–48.

Canzoneri, Robert. *A Highly Ramified Tree: An American Writer Returns to His Father's Roots in Sicily*. New York: Viking, 1976.

Capozzi, F. C. *Protestantism and the Latin Soul*. Philadelphia: John C. Winston Company, 1918.

———. "Where I Found God." Manuscript, courtesy of Anthony Baker (descendant of Capozzi). Undated, c. 1955.

Carnevali, Emanuel. *The Autobiography of Emanuel Carnevali*. Edited by Kay Boyle. New York: Horizon Press, 1967.

———. "The Return." *Furnished Rooms*. Edited by Dennis Barone. New York: Bordighera Press, 2006, 70–74.

Carr, John Foster. *Guide to the United States for the Immigrant Italian*. Garden City, New York: Doubleday, 1911.

Cautela, Giuseppe. "Italian Funeral." *American Mercury* October, 1928: 200–206.

"Certificate of Identification: Alfredo Barone." United States Department of Justice. February 17, 1942. Collection of the author.

"Chiropractor's Case Reported to the Coroner." *Bridgeport Evening Farmer* April 24, 1913, 1.

Chivers, E. E. "Our Baptist Italian Mission Work." *Baptist Home Mission Monthly* 27.5 (May 1905): 187–200.

Choate, Mark I. *Emigrant Nation: The Making of Italy Abroad*. Cambridge, MA: Harvard University Press, 2008.

"Church Anniversary." *Hartford Courant* July 24, 1905, 4.

"Church Birthday Party." *Hartford Courant* July 18, 1904, 7.

Cipolla, Benedicta. "My Father, the Priest." *New York Times* September 20, 2015, SR8.

"The City Churches and What They Do." *Hartford Courant* January 17, 1912, 10.

"City, Country, Family, Church: A Story of St. John Presbyterian Institutional Church." Chicago: St. John Presbyterian Institutional Church, 1936. Chicago History Museum, Chicago, Illinois.

"City Mission Building." *Hartford Courant* March 28, 1904, 2.

"City Mission's Home." *Hartford Courant* April 28, 1904, 13.

Claghorn, Kate Holladay. "Our Italian Immigrants." *Baptist Home Mission Monthly* 27.5 (May 1905): 177–182.
"Columbus Day to Be Observed Here in Varied Commemorative Program." *Hartford Courant* October 12, 1938, 1.
"Conference Will Aid Suffering Jews." *Hartford Courant* November 16, 1905, 14.
"Connecticut Is a 'Foreign State.'" *Hartford Courant* June 1, 1905, 5.
Contract for Alfred Barone. Joseph Cuva Monumental Works, Stamford, CT, July, 1925. Collection of the author.
Coroner's Report. Fairfield County Cornoner Records, vol. 30, 1912–1913: 365–366. Connecticut State Library, Hartford, CT.
"Corriere Delle Nostre Missioni: Castelbaroni e Trevico." *Il Testimonio* April 1894: 3. Unione Cristiana Battista d'Italia, Rome, Italy.
Covello, Leonard with Guido D'Agostino. *The Heart Is the Teacher*. New York: McGraw-Hill, 1958.
Culler, Jonathan. *Structuralist Poetics: Structuralism, Linguistics, and the Study of Literature*. Ithaca, NY: Cornell University Press, 1975.
D'Agostino, Peter. "The Religious Life of Italians in New York." *The Italians of New York: Five Centuries of Struggle and Achievement*. Edited by Philip V. Cannistraro. New York: The New-York Historical Society and the John D. Calandra Italian American Institute, 2000, 69–75.
———. *Rome in America: Transnational Catholic Ideology from the Risorgimento to Fascism*. Chapel Hill: University of North Carolina Press, 2004.
D'Alfonso, Antonio. E-mail correspondence to Dennis Barone. September 24, 2003.
D'Angelo, Pascal. *Son of Italy*. 1924. Toronto: Guernica Editions, 2003.
Decker, Robert Owen. *Hartford Immigrants: A History of the Christian Activities Council (Congregational) 1850–1980*. New York: United Church Press, 1987.
De Luise, Alexandra. "Mission Work, Conversion, and the Italian Immigrant in Turn-of-the-Century New York City." Paper delivered at the annual meeting of the Italian American Studies Association, New Orleans, October 4, 2013.
Demos, John. *The Heathen School: A Story of Hope and Betrayal in the Age of the Early Republic*. New York: Knopf, 2014.
Di Domenica, Angelo. "Interesting Italian Work." *Baptist Home Mission Monthly* 24.8 (August 1902): 231.
———. *Protestant Witness of a New American: Mission of a Lifetime*. Philadelphia: Judson Press, 1956.
———. "The Sons of Italy in America." *Missionary Review of the World* 41 (March 1918): 189–195.

———. "St. John's Baptist Church." *Golden Anniversary Annual of the Italian Baptist Association of America, 1898-1948*: 31-32. Historical Society of Pennsylvania. Philadelphia.

Di Domenica, Vincenzo. "Blessing and Opposition." *The Baptist Home Mission Monthly* 24.8 (August 1902): 231.

Di Donato, Pietro. *Christ in Concrete*. 1939. New York: Penguin, 1993.

———. *Immigrant Saint: The Life of Mother Cabrini*. 1960. New York: St. Martin's Press, 1991.

Di Sano, Carmelo. "The American Church and the Mission Among Italians in America." *La Sentinella* October 1925: 3-5.

"Does This Appeal to You?" *Baptist Home Mission Monthly* 29.9 (1907): 358.

Dorcas Society Cookbook. Monson, MA: Congregational Church, 1906. Monson Historical Society.

"Dr. Aniello Preziosi." *Stamford Advocate* May 26, 1910, 1.

"East Side Folks." *Hartford Courant* February 15, 1904, 6.

Eaton, William Harrison. *Historical Sketch of the Massachusetts Baptist Missionary Society and Convention: 1802-1902*. Boston: Massachusetts Baptist Convention, 1903.

"Estratto Dell 'Atto di Nascita N. 546, 1869, Salerno." Servizi Demografica, Comune di Salerno, Italy.

Farnham, Edwin. "Rev. Antonio Mangano." *Baptist Home Mission Monthly* 29 (September 1907): 317-318.

Federazione della Chiese Evangeliche in Italia website. www.fedevangelica.it. Accessed December 3, 2013.

"Fifty Years of Work." *Hartford Courant* November 25, 1901, 1, 10.

"Fight in Monson Quarries." *Hartford Courant* April 4, 1893, 1.

"Formal Reception by Italian Church Thursday Night." *Hartford Courant* February 2, 1937, 20.

"Freeing of Italy Celebrated Here." *Hartford Courant* September 20, 1920, 4.

Frisina, Annalisa. "The Making of Religious Pluralism in Italy: Discussing Religious Education from a New Generational Perspective." *Social Compass* 58.2 (2011): 271-284.

Galgano, Luigi. E-mail message to Dennis Barone. November 30, 2014.

Garibaldi, Giuseppe. *The Rule of the Monk; or, Rome in the Nineteenth Century*. 1867. London: Cassell, Petter and Galpin, n.d.

"The 'General Conference.'" *The Hartford Courant* October 18, 1905, 8.

Giampetruzzi, Marco. E-mail correspondence to Dennis Barone, May 5, 2012.

Giornale dei Processi Verbali della Confraternita di San Paolo, 1928-1956. Archives. Episcopal Diocese of Connecticut, Meriden, CT.

"Good Living Best Teacher Pastor Says." *Hartford Courant* April 22, 1929, 3.

Gordon, Richard E., Katherine K. Gordon, and Max Gunther. *The Split-Level Trap*. 1960. New York: Dell, 1964.

Gramsci, Antonio. *The Southern Question*. 1930. Translated by Pasquale Verdicchio. West Lafayette, IN: Bordighera Press, 1995.

"Granddaughter of Italy's Liberator." *Hartford Courant* September 12, 1910, 13.

Grant, Madison. *The Passing of the Great Race or The Radical Bias of European History*. New York: Scribner's Sons, 1916.

Grass, Gunter. *Two States—One Nation?* Translated by Krishna Winston. San Diego: Harcourt, 1990.

Grose, Howard B. *Aliens or Americans?* New York: Young People's Missionary Movement, 1909.

———. *The Incoming Millions*. New York: Revell, 1906.

Hayne, Coe. "Highways to the Friendly Heart." *Missions: American Baptist International Magazine* April 1924: 210–212; May 1924: 276–278; June 1924: 351–353.

Hendin, Josephine Gattuso. *The Right Thing to Do*. 1988. New York: The Feminist Press, 1999.

Herberg, Will. *Protestant, Catholic, Jew: An Essay in American Religious Sociology*. Garden City, New York: Double Day, 1955.

"Historical Administrative Note." Coll. 2624. Chestnut Street Methodist Church. Maine Historical Society. Portland, Maine.

Hollinger, David. *Postethnic America: Beyond Multiculturalism*. New York: Basic Books, 1995.

"Home Missionary Work." *Hartford Courant* April 19, 1899, 5.

"Hotel Guests Are Asked to Church." *Hartford Courant* April 25, 1908, 4.

"How the Home Mission Work Spreads." *Baptist Home Mission Monthly* 29.1 (January 1907): 43.

Howells, William Dean. *Italian Journeys*. New York: Hurd and Houghton, 1867.

"An Interesting Career: How a Shoe Factory Boy Became a Student and Minister." *Baptist Home Mission Monthly* 30.11 (November, 1908): 449.

"Italian Baptist Church." *Journal Register* (Palmer, MA) October 21, 1904, 1.

"Italian Baptist Church Dedicated." *Springfield Republican* April 30, 1928, 4.

"Italian Freedom Theme of Speeches." *The Hartford Courant* September 21, 1914, 15.

"Italian Immigrants." *Hartford Courant* October 24, 1903, 7.

"Italian Mission at Monson, Mass.," *Baptist Home Mission Monthly* 27.4 (April 1905): 141.

Italian Mission Reports, 1900–1909. International Mission Board. Unione Cristiana Evangelica Battista d'Italia, Rome, Italy.

"The Italian People Who Live in Hartford." *Hartford Courant* April 24, 1910, X1.

"The Italian Theological School." *Baptist Home Mission Monthly* 29 (Feb. 1907): 447.

"Italian Unity Celebrated." *Hartford Courant* September 19, 1904, 4.
"Italians—New Haven, Conn." *Baptist Home Mission Monthly* 24 (October 1902): 282.
Ives, Joel S. "The Gospel for the Italians." *Home Missionary* 77.9 (December 1903): 332–333.
———. "Italian Connecticut." *Home Missionary* 78.8 (January 1905): 301–303.
———. "Italy in Connecticut." *Home Missionary* 82.7 (December 1908): 607–608.
King, Henry M. "An Italian's Confession of Faith." *Baptist Home Mission Monthly* 26.2 (February 1904): 46–47.
Labanca, Baldassare. *Gesù Cristo nella letteratura contemporanea, straniera e italiana*. Torino: Fratelli Bocca, 1903.
Landells, W. "Remarks on the Italian Mission." Regent's Park College Archives, Oxford, England.
Lapolla, Garibaldi M. *The Grand Gennaro*. New York: Vanguard, 1933.
Lee, Samuel H. "Italian Characteristics." *The Baptist Home Mission Monthly* 27.5 (1905): 183–185.
"The Legacy of a Beloved Minister." http://www.marblechurch.org/AboutUs/History/DrArthurCaliandro/tabid/308/Default.aspx. Accessed January 9, 2013.
Levi, Carlo. *Christ Stopped at Eboli: The Story of a Year*. 1945. Translated by Frances Frenaye. New York: Farrar, Straus and Giroux, 2006.
Luconi, Stefano. "Fascism and Italian-American Politics." *Italian Americana* 33.1 (2015): 6–24.
Luzzi, Giovanni. *The Struggle for Christian Truth in Italy*. New York: Revell, 1913.
———. "Three Romantic Chapters in the History of the Italian Bible." *Biblical Review* 2 (1917): 289–309.
Macnab, John B. "Bethlehem Chapel: Presbyterians and Italian Americans in New York City." *Journal of Presbyterian History* 55.2 (1977): 145–160.
Mandrano, Maura. E-mail correspondence with Dennis Barone. February 11–18, 2014.
Mangano, Antonio. "The Closing of the Italian Department of the Colgate-Rochester Divinity School." (ca. 1932). Manuscript, Special Collections and University Archives, Colgate University Libraries.
———. "Expansion and Duty: Commencement Speech." 1899. Manuscript, University Archives, Brown University, Providence, Rhode Island.
———. *Religious Work Among Italians in America*. New York: Missionary Education Movement, 1917.
———. *Sons of Italy: A Social and Religious Study of Italians in America*. 1917. Whitefish, MT: Kessinger Publishing, 2007.
Mangione, Jerre. *An Ethnic at Large: A Memoir of America in the Thirties and Forties*. 1978. Syracuse: Syracuse University Press, 2001.

———. *Mount Allegro: A Memoir of Italian American Life*. 1942. Syracuse: Syracuse University Press, 1998.
"Massachusetts–Monson." *The Baptist Home Mission Monthly* 23.10 (October 1901): 286–287.
"Mayor Henney Speaks to Hartford Italians." *Hartford Courant* September 25, 1905, 11.
McLeod, Christian (Anna Ruddy). *The Heart of a Stranger: A Story of Little Italy*. New York: Revell, 1908.
Meehan, Thomas F. "Evangelizing the Italians." *The Messenger* Fifth Series, vol. 3 (1903): 16–32.
Mercadante, Linda. *Bloomfield Avenue: A Jewish-Catholic Jersey Girl's Spiritual Journey*. Cambridge, MA: Cowley Publications, 2006.
———. "'My Conversion and Aspiration': A Comparative Case, Constantine Panunzio." *Italian Americana* 27.2 (2008): 137–146.
"Minister Declares Italian Republic Gains Acceptance." *Hartford Courant* September 28, 1948, 6.
"Minister to Italians Is Reluctant to Retire." *Hartford Courant* May 1, 1976, 19.
Minutes of the Meetings of the Committee in Charge of St. Paul's Italian Mission, May 1920 to December 31, 1921. Archives. Episcopal Diocese of Connecticut, Meriden, CT.
Minutes of the Westfield Baptist Association, 1904–1910. American Baptist Historical Society, Atlanta, Georgia.
"Monson." *Springfield Republican* July 13, 1910, 10.
Monson Historical Society. *The History of Monson, Massachusetts*. Monson, MA: Monson Historical Society, 1960.
Murphy, Jim. *Pick & Shovel Poet: The Journeys of Pascal D'Angelo*. New York: Clarion Books, 2000.
"Natale Ricciardi Dies; Led Church in Hartford." *Hartford Courant* April 14, 1984, B8.
"New Pastor Appointed at First Italian." *Hartford Courant* May 22, 1931, 28.
"New Village St. Mission." *Hartford Courant* April 23, 1904, 4.
Newton, Riccardo. *Gli Animali Della Bibbia e le Lezioni Che Ci Danno*. Translated by Giovanni Luzzi. Florence: Tipografia Claudiana, 1891.
Notes from 1912 pamphlet. 1900–1920 Binder One, Archives of the Italian Baptist Church of Meriden, First Baptist Church of Wallingford. Memorial Parish House, Wallingford, CT.
Opacum Land Trust. "Helping to Preserve Nature and History in Monson." www.opacumlt.org. Accessed November 11, 2009.
Orsi, Robert Anthony. *The Madonna of 115th Street: Faith and Community in Italian Harlem, 1880–1950*. New Haven: Yale University Press, 1985.
Pace, Enzo. "A Peculiar Pluralism." *Journal of Modern Italian Studies* 12.1 (2007): 86–100.

Palmieri, F. Aurelio. "Italian Protestantism in the United States." *The Catholic World* 107 (May 1918): 177–189.
Palminota, Nunzio. "Calitri." *Il Testimonio* December 1955: 453–456. Unione Cristiana Battista d'Italia, Rome, Italy.
Panunzio, Constantine. *The Soul of an Immigrant*. New York: Macmillan, 1921.
Parati, Graziella. *Migration Italy: The Art of Talking Back in a Destination Culture*. Toronto: University of Toronto Press, 2005.
"Pastor Installed." *Hartford Courant* July 9, 1903, 7.
Peale, Norman Vincent. *The Power of Positive Thinking*. 1952. NY: Simon & Schuster, 2003.
Pirazzini, Agide. "Training an Italian Ministry for America." *Protestant Evangelism Among Italians in America*. Edited by Francesco Cordasco. New York: Arno Press, 1975, 152–153.
Plasse, Eugene. "St. Monica's Mission." Palmer, MA: St. Thomas Church, 2008.
Prior, Charles E. "Italian Baptist Mission, Hartford, Conn." *Watchman* February 4, 1909, 9–11.
Puzo, Mario. *The Fortunate Pilgrim*. 1964. New York: Ballantine, 1998.
Report of the Committee on Americanization. Brooklyn: Italian Baptist Missionary Association, 1918.
"Rev. Antonio Roca Ordained." *Hartford Courant* April 29, 1903, 5.
Riesman, David. *The Lonely Crowd: A Study of the Changing American Character*. New Haven: Yale University Press, 1950.
"Rocky Hill." *Hartford Courant* March 6, 1906, 16.
Rose, Philip M. *Congregational Work Among Italians in America*. New York: The Congregational Home Missionary Society, 1918.
Ruberto, Laura E. "Always Italian, Still Foreign: Connecting Women's Lives Through Transnational Migration." *La Questione Meridionale* 2 (2011): 77–97.
Saggio, Joseph J. "A Brief History of Italian Pentecostalism in America." *AG Heritage* 2010: 35–41.
Sartorio, Enrico C. *Social and Religious Life of Italians in America*. Boston: Christopher Publishing House, 1918.
Scalise, Charles J. "'My Conversion and Aspiration': The Protestant Americanization of Angelo di Domenica, 1872–1970." *Italian Americana* 27.2 (2008): 125–136.
———. "Retrieving the 'WIPS': Exploring the Assimilation of White Italian Protestants in America." *Italian Americana* 24.2 (2006): 136–146.
"A School of Prophets: Pageant of Italian Baptist Work and Training School in America." (ca. 1928). Manuscript. Special Collections and University Archives, Colgate University Libraries.
Serra, Ilaria. *The Value of Worthless Lives: Writing Italian American Immigrant Autobiographies*. New York: Fordham University Press, 2007.

Sheffield, Mariagrazia. E-mail correspondence with Dennis Barone. January 16–October 4, 2014.
Skinner, Lilian M. "Our Italian Neighbors." *Neighbors: Studies in Immigration from the Standpoint of the Episcopal Church*. Edited by W. C. Sturgis. New York: Domestic and Foreign Missionary Society, 1919, 85–108.
Snow, Wilbert. "Connecticut Tercentenary Ode." *The Collected Poems of Wilbert Snow*. Middletown, CT: Wesleyan University Press, 1963, 147–151.
Speranza, Gino. *Race or Nation: A Conflict of Divided Loyalties*. 1923. Indianapolis: Bobbs-Merrill, 1925.
Spini, Giorgio. *Risorgimento e protestanti*. Torino: Claudiana, 1989.
"St. Paul's Italian Church." (Printed Informational Report, ca. 1925.) Archives. Episcopal Diocese of Connecticut, Meriden, CT.
"St. Paul's Italian Episcopal Mission. Hartford, Conn." *La Croce* 40 (July 1915): 1–3. Archives. Episcopal Diocese of Connecticut, Meriden, CT.
Stone, George M. "The Italian Mission in Hartford." *Watchman* October 31, 1907: 21.
"Summer Work of Local Churches." *Hartford Courant* July 4, 1908, 4.
Swierad, Mary. E-mail message to Dennis Barone. March 25, 2010.
"To Talk About Italians." *Hartford Courant* February 18, 1904, 3.
Tanguay, Christopher. "St. Monica's Mission Complete." *Sturbridge Villager* September 5, 2008: 1, 11.
Tanzilo, Robert. "The Battle for Souls: A Protestant Evangelist in Italian Milwaukee." *Italian Americana* 23.2 (2005): 201–224.
Taylor, George B. *Italy and the Italians*. Philadelphia: American Baptist Publication Society, 1898.
Taylor, George Braxton, ed. *Life and Letters of Rev. George Boardman Taylor, D. D.* Lynchburg, VA: J. P. Bell, 1908.
Taylor, George Braxton. *Southern Baptist in Sunny Italy*. New York: Walter Neale, 1929.
"Telegraphic Brevities." *New York Times* April 21, 1891, 2.
Tennent, Gilbert. *The Blessedness of Peace-Makers represented; and the Dangers of Persecution considered*. Philadelphia: William Bradford, 1765.
———. *The Danger of an Unconverted Ministry*. Philadelphia: Benjamin Franklin, 1740.
———. *A Solemn Warning to the Secure World, From the God of Terrible Majesty*. Boston: Printed by S. Kneeland and T. Green, for D. Henchman, 1735.
———. "Thoughts on Extempore Preaching." Manuscript. Presbyterian Historical Society, Philadelphia, PA.
Tolino, John V. "The Church in America and the Italian Problem." *American Ecclesiastical Review* 100 (January 1939): 22–32.

Treasurer, St. Paul's Italian Mission. Fundraising Letter. May 26, 1943. Archives. Episcopal Diocese of Connecticut, Meriden, CT.

Tresca, Carlo. *The Autobiography of Carlo Tresca*. Edited by Nunzio Pernicone. New York: The Calandra Italian American Institute, 2003.

"Trouble in East Side Revival." *The Hartford Courant* October 24, 1910, 3.

Turco, Lewis. "Father and Son." *Shaking the Family Tree*. West Lafayette, IN: Bordighera Press, 1998, 32–48.

———. Letter to Dennis Barone. November 18, 2012.

Turco, Luigi. "A Brief Story of My Life." *The Spiritual Autobiography of Luigi Turco*. Edited by Lewis Turco. Minneapolis: Center for Immigration Studies at the University of Minnesota, 1969, 1–14.

———. "Man, Know Thyself." Manuscript. Immigration History Center. University of Minnesota, Minneapolis, Minnesota.

———. "Postscript: A Letter to My Son." *The Spiritual Autobiography of Luigi Turco*. Edited by Lewis Turco. Minneapolis: Center for Immigration Studies at the University of Minnesota, 1969, 230–244.

———. "The Redemption of the Body." Manuscript. Immigration History Center. University of Minnesota, Minneapolis.

———. "The Wisdom of the Bible." *The Spiritual Autobiography of Luigi Turco*. Edited by Lewis Turco. Minneapolis: Center for Immigration Studies at the University of Minnesota, 1969, 15–229.

———. "Your Silent Partner." Manuscript. Immigration History Center. University of Minnesota, Minneapolis.

"Untitled Repudiation of Remarks by the Rev. W. Landells D.D. on the Italian Mission, Addressed to Baynes." 1892. Regent's Park College Archives, Oxford, England.

Van Nest, A. R. "The Holy Catholic Church." *Report of the American Union Church*. Florence, Italy: Claudian Press, 1872, 3–10.

Vasquez, Paolo. Letter to the Dean of Christ Church Cathedral. February 12, 1925. Archives. Episcopal Diocese of Connecticut, Meriden, CT.

———. "Report of St. Paul's Italian Mission." 1943. Manuscript. Archives, Episcopal Diocese of Connecticut, Meriden, CT.

Venturi, Robert. "Upbringing Among Quakers." *Growing Up Italian*. Edited by Linda Brandi Cateura. New York: Morrow, 1987: 194–201.

Villari, Luigi. *Italian Life in Town and Country*. New York: Putnam's, 1902.

Vizzini, Paul. E-mail correspondence with Dennis Barone. June 4–6, 2009.

Wacker, Grant. *Heaven Below: Early Pentecostals and American Culture*. Cambridge: Harvard University Press, 2003.

Walker, Robert. "Corriere Delle Nostre Missioni: Calitri." *Il Testimonio* November 1892: 3. Unione Cristiana Battista d'Italia, Rome, Italy.

———. Letter with Plan to Mr. Baynes. May 20, 1899. Regent's Park College Archives, Oxford, England.

———. Letters to Mr. Baynes. 1889-1900. Regent's Park College Archives, Oxford, England.

Ward, Michael T. "Waldensians in Texas: Religious Assimilation in Galveston and Wolf Ridge." *Italian Immigrants Go West: The Impact of Locale on Ethnicity*. Edited by Janet E. Worrall, Carol Bonomo Albright, and Elvira G. Di Fabio. Cambridge: American Italian Historical Association, 2003, 194-206.

Wassef, Nadine. "Review of *18 Ius soli*." *Italian American Review* 3.1 (2013): 82-85.

Watt, Jon C. "The Italian Pentecostal Movement: An Italian American Response to Irish Hegemony in American Catholicism at the Turn of the Twentieth Century." *Italian Immigrants Go West: The Impact of Locale on Ethnicity*. Edited by Janet E. Worrall, Carol Bonomo Albright, and Elvira G. Di Fabio. Cambridge: American Italian Historical Association, 2003, 176-193.

Waugh, Evelyn. *The Loved One*. 1948. NY: Little, Brown and Company, 2012.

Whittinghill, D. G. "Baptist Work and Prospects in Italy." *The Review and Expositor* 11.3 (July 1914): 323-350.

———. "The Italian Mission." *Southern Baptist Foreign Missions*. Edited by T. Bronson Ray. Nashville: Sunday School Board Southern Baptist Convention, 1910: 148-173.

Wilson, Tracey. "From Steno Pool to Factory Floor." *Connecticut Explored* 12.1 (2013/14): 38-43.

Index

Abbate, William, 61, 100, 110
Abel, Theodore, 28, 77
African American community, 127–128
Aliens or Americans (Grose), 96
Alpha and Omega Assembly, 20, 97, 145
American Church (Florence, Italy), 113
Americanization
  adapting to customs, 120–121
  desire for, 133
  evangelization and, 40, 104
  Italian identity and, 139–140
  religion and, 4–5, 26–27, 58–59, 63–65
  See also Conversion to Protestantism; Literacy of immigrants
American Union Church (Florence), 41
Angell, James Rowland, 104
Anglo American Protestants, 79, 107–108, 145–146
Anti-Catholic sentiment, 22, 24–26
Antimodernism of Catholic Church, 52–53, 80–81
Aprile, Pino, 50–51
Arrighi, Antonio, 21, 24–25, 39, 44, 46, 71–74

Asylum Hill Congregational Church, 106
Auster, Paul, 18
Autobiographies, 33
  See also specific authors

Baptist Church, Italian. *See* Italian Baptist Churches
Baptist Foreign Mission Board, 45
Barolini, Helen, 17–18, 32, 34
Barone, Alfredo
  Alpha and Omega Assembly, 20, 97, 145
  birth, 85, 143
  children of, 5, 23, 35, 80, 85
  as chiropractor, 142–143
  contemporaries of, 81–83
  death, 80, 85, 96–97
  emigration to America, 82, 83, 92–93
  evangelizing, 10, 47, 88–91
  grave of, 152–153
  great-grandson speaking about, 1–3
  as inspiring influence, 97
  Italian identity of, 6, 139–140
  life after emigrating, 87–88
  The Life of Jesus Christ or the Harmony of the Gospels, 37–38, 86–87

Barone, Alfredo *(continued)*
  married life, 145–146
  ministries after Monson, 5–6, 98
  in Monson, 18–19, 94–97
  persecutions experienced by, 3,
    12, 22, 38–39, 85, 91–92
  photographs, Figure 3, Figure 4,
    Figure 5
  relationship with parents, 12, 22,
    143–145
  religious development, 23
  on requirements for ministers,
    122–123
  Sannella and, 38, 46–47
  Springfield Republican notice, 112
Barone, Giovanni (John), 35, 92–93,
  143
Barone, Melchisedec, 35, 80
Barone, Rosina, 143–145, 152–153
Barton, Bruce, 35
Bellondi, Ariel, 62
Belotti, Elena Gianini, 70–71
Bencivenni, Marcella, 52
Bible
  distribution of, 33
  Jesus's teachings on the Church,
    114
  ministers studying, 123
  Protestants reading, 133, 137
  references to church, 113
  role in conversions, 53
*Bible Animals and Lessons Taught by
  Them* (Newton), 35
Bible Mystery and Bible Meaning
  (Troward), 127–128
The Bitter Tast of Strangers' Bread
  (Belotti), 70–71
Bowler, Kate, 128, 137
Branch churches, 121–122
Bridge and devil parable, 72–73
Brodhead, Richard, 106
Bruno, Guinio, 81–83

Business and material aspirations,
  130–131
Butler, Willis H., 106

Cabrini, Francesca, 74–76
Caliandro, Arthur, 8–9, 117, 120,
  132–139, Figure 7
Calitri, Antonio, 81–83
Calitri, Charles, 81–83
Calitri, Italy
  Barone's impact on, 86–87
  as center for spiritual awakening,
    85–86
  church of, 88
  evangelizing in, 88–91
  pull of, 149
Cannistraro, Philip, 19
Canzoneri, Robert, 26
Capozzi, Francis Clement, 53, 59
Card playing, 25
Carnevali, Emanuel, 101–102
Carr, John Foster, 110
Catholic Church
  Americans' views on Italians and,
    77–78, 105–106, 133
  antimodernism of, 52–53, 80–
    81
  Fascism and, 54, 119, 124, 148
  innateness of Catholic faith to
    Italians, 77–78
  Madonna Chapel, 95–96
  opposing Protestantism, 91
  power of, 93
  Protestantism comparison, 90–91
  religious education in Italian
    schools, 79–80, 147–148
  return to, 149–150
  sentiments against, 22, 24–26
  Socialism and, 52
  state funds for Catholic school/
    orphanage, 79–80
  statues of saints, 82

struggles of Protestants with, 39, 54–55, 92
Catholic priests
  Calitri (Antonio) as, 82–83
  charging for burial service, 61
  ex-priests as Protestant missionaries, 81
  faith of, 71–74
  as former Episcopal priests, 149–150
Cautela, Giuseppe, 111
Cerreta, Donato, 89
Chestnut Street Church, 131
Chiesa Apostolica Battista, 95, 98, Figure 3
  See also Monson Italian Baptist Church
Chiminelli, Piero, 111
Choate, Mark I., 20, 26, 29, 40
Christ for Italy, 98
Christ in Concrete (di Donato), 75–76
Christ Stopped at Eboli (Levi), 51
Cipolla, Benedicta, 149–150
Claghorn, Kate Holladay, 60
Clarke, Edward, 90
Codella, Pasquale, 64
Colgate University, 123–124, 126–127
Colonial Revival, 62
Colonizers' attitudes, 116
Colton, Olcott B., 102–103
Congregational Churches, 61, 62, 106
  See also Italian Congregational Church
Congregational Home Missionary Society, 104–105
Conversion to Protestantism
  assimilation and, 5–7
  benefits for immigrants, 17
  difficulties of, 92
  of friends and family, 23–24
  Mangano (Antonio) on, 21, 41, 57–58, 78, 114–118
  of ministers, 5, 24–26
  role of Bible in, 53
  settings for, 23–24
  See also Americanization; Evangelization
Cooperation between congregations, 121–122
Covello, Leonard, 19
Creanza, Michele, 87
Criminal sensationalism, 27–28
Cultural amnesia, 63
Culture of Italy, 109

D'Agostino, Peter R., 40, 67–68
D'Albergo, Arturo, 23
D'Angelo, Pascal, 11, 13
The Danger of an Unconverted Ministry (Tennent), 117–118
Davis, F. Irwin, 106
De Carlo, Pasquale, 64, 101–106, 108
Decker, Robert Owen, 107
Demos, John, 151–152
di Domenica, Angelo, 21, 23–27, 35, 58, 77–78, 79–80, 119, 121
di Domenica, Vincenzo (Vincent), 87, 141–142, Figure 5
di Donato, Pietro, 74–76
di Lampedusa, Giuseppe Tomasi, 93
Di Sano, Carmelo, 148
Discrimination against Italians, 107–108, 133–134
  See also Persecution

Eaton, William Harrison, 94
Eddy, Mary Baker, 127–128
Education
  in Italian schools, 79–80, 147–148
  for ministers, 122–124

170 Index

Education *(continued)*
  theology schools, 45, 123–124, 126–127
  See also Language
Emigration
  of Barone (Alfredo), 82, 83, 92–93
  of 1890s, 56–57, 92
Emotional appeals *vs.* reason, 117–119, 136
English Baptist Mission, 89, 92
Episcopal Church, 53, 59, 150
An Ethnic at Large (Mangione), 31
Evangelization
  Americanization and, 40, 104
  of Barone (Alfredo), 10, 47, 88–91
  in Calitri, Italy, 88–91
  expansionist policies and, 115–116
  finding ministers, 45
  messages to non-Protestant audiences, 114–115
  methods of, 135
  as propaganda, 119
  reason *vs.* emotional appeals, 117–119
  at tent meetings, 119–120, 141–142
  volatile era in Italy, 43–47
  See also Conversion to Protestantism; Missions and missionaries
Expansionism of U.S., 115–116

Farnham, Edwin P., 115–116
Fascism, 54, 119, 124, 148
Father (Calitri), 81–83
Federation of Protestant Churches in Italy, 146–147
Ferretti, Salvatore, 41
First Presbyterian Church, 149
Flynt Quarry, 93–95
The Fortunate Pilgrim (Puzo), 17, 32–33, 34

Frisina, Annalisa, 147

Garibaldi, Giuseppe, 24, 54, 69, 100
Geographic movement of missionaries, 141
Gill, Everette, 42
Giuffrida, Rolando, 49
Global perspective, 151–152
Gordon, Katherine K., 125–126, 129–130
Gordon, Richard E., 125–126, 129–130
Gramsci, Antonio, 52
The Grand Gennaro (LaPolla), 19
Granone, Antonio, 101
Grant, Madison, 35
Grose, Howard B., 60, 94–95, 96
Guide to the Immigrant Italian (Carr), 110
Guiliani, August, 118
Gunther, Max, 125–126, 129–130

Hartford attitudes toward Italian immigrants
  celebrating Italian identity, 109–110
  on citizenship, 103–104
  discrimination, 107–108
  viewing cooperation, 100–102
  viewing customs, 102–103
  viewing religion, 105–107
Hartford Episcopal Italian Mission, 28–29
Hayne, Coe, 59
The Heart of a Stranger (Ruddy), 17, 27–28
The Heathen School (Demos), 151–152
Hendin, Josephine Gattuso, 68–70
Hollinger, David A., 132
Holmes, Ernest, 127, 128
Howells, William Dean, 90–91

Illiteracy of immigrants, 20
Immanuel Congregational Church, 110
Immigrants
  conversion to Protestantism benefiting, 21
  exposed to Protestantism, 50
  right to citizenship, 148–149
  See also Americanization; Irish Americans; Italian Protestants; Language
Immigrant Saint (di Donato), 74–76
In His Steps (Sheldon), 35
Institutionalization
  American attitudes toward Italian immigrants, 120–121
  branch churches, 121–122
  education for ministers, 122–124
Intensive stage of religious work. *See* Transformation as stage of religious work
Intolerance. *See* Persecution
Irish Americans
  conflicts with Italian Catholics, 68–70
  discriminating against Italians, 141–142
  poor treatment of Italians by priests and nuns, 149
  troubled by Italian customs, 76
Italian Baptist Churches
  in Hartford (CT), 100
  in Lawrence (MA), 62
  Like the Salt of the Earth (DVD), 88
  in Meriden (CT), 49, 127
  in Monson (MA), 18–19, 31–32, 46–47, 93–98, 142–143, Figure 4
  in Philadelphia, 121
  purposes of, 124
  in Stamford (CT), 64, 87, Figure 5
  statistics, 4

Italian Catholic Church of New Haven, 79–80
Italian Catholics. *See* Catholic Church; Catholic priests
Italian Congregational Church
  in Bridgeport (CT), 87, Figure 2
  in Hartford (CT), 8, 60–62, 64, 99–100, 106–107, 109, 111, 151
  See also Congregational Churches
Italian customs, 76, 102–103
Italian Department of Colgate University, 9, 123–124, 126–127
Italian identity, 109–110, 139–140, 147–149
Italian language, 26, 110
Italian Protestants
  Catholic Church persecuting, 91
  church enrollment, 4, 78–79
  fluidity of affiliations, 87–88
  generalizations about, 150–151
  joining nonethnically specialized churches, 63–65
  ministers working with Anglo-Protestant ministers, 79
  overlooked, 11
  requirements for ministers, 122–123
  See also Persecution; *specific denominations*
Italy and the Italians (Taylor), 45
Ives, Joel S., 58, 79, 104, 106, 140, Fig. 1

Jesus Christ in Contemporary Literature, Foreign and Italian (Labanca), 86–87

Labanca, Baldassare, 86–87
Landells, W., 44
Landowners and laborers, conflicts between, 56

172   Index

Language
  English proficiency, 32
  Italian, 26, 110
  literacy of immigrants, 33, 57, 90, 111
LaPolla, Garibaldi M., 19
Lee, Samuel H., 97
Leo, Pope, 68
Levi, Carlo, 51–52
The Life of Jesus Christ or the Harmony of the Gospels (Barone), 37–38, 86–87
Like the Salt of the Earth (DVD), 88
Lisi, Gaetano, 96
Literacy of immigrants, 33, 57, 90, 111
Literary sources, 11–12
  See also specific sources
Loneliness, 130
Lost and Found (Caliandro), 133–134, 137
The Lost World of Italian-American Radicalism (Cannistraro and Meyer), 19–20
Love, sermon on, 138
Luzzi, Giovanni, 40–41, 55–56

Madonna Chapel, 95–96
Maffei, Anna, 2
Make Your Life Count (Caliandro), 134
Mandrano, Maura, 149
Mangano, Antonio
  on branch churches, 121–122
  on Christian work, 63, 142
  at Colgate Theological Seminary, 126–127
  Hartford Episcopal Italian Mission, 28–29
  Italian Department of Colgate University, 123–124
  marriage, 145
  on modernism, 81
  on persecution, 54
  photographs, Figure 6
  on Protestant conversion, 21, 41, 57–58, 78, 114–118
  stages of religious work, 124–125
Mangione, Jerre, 31–32
The Man Nobody Knows (Barton), 35
Marble Collegiate Church, 120, 132–135, 138–139
Maselli, Domenico, 2
Material aspirations, 130–131, 140
Mazzini, Giuseppe, 55
Meehan, Thomas F., 102
Mercadante, Linda, 6
Meriden Church, 57
Merlino, Giuseppe, 102, 105
Methodist Episcopal Church Mission (Bologna), 72
Methodists of Portland, Maine, 131, 133
Meyer, Gerald, 19–20
Milwaukee Italian Evangelical Church, 118–119
Missions and missionaries, 27–30, 42
Modernism, 80–81
Monson Congregational Church, 96, 152
Monson Italian Baptist Church, 18–19, 31–32, 46–47, 93–98, 142–143, Figure 3, Figure 4
Mount Allegro (Mangione), 31–32
Music, 27–28, 120, 133

National identity of Italy, 109–110, 139–140, 147–149
National Italian Heritage Month, 64
Native American Protestants. *See* Anglo American Protestants
Naylor, Louis H., 112
New Thought Movement, 8, 128–130, 137

Newton, Richard, 35
New York City Baptist Mission Society, 38
Northern and Southern Italy, comparison of, 60
North-South division of Italy, 52–57

Open-air evangelization, 119–120, 141–142
Orsi, Robert, 19, 76

Pace, Enzo, 147–148
Paladino, Joseph, 61
Palmieri, Aurelio, 22, 77, 104
Palminota, Nunzio, 85, 87
Panunzio, Constantine M., 17, 22–23, 25–26, 30–31
Parable of the bridge and devil, 72–73
Parati, Graziella, 9, 141
Patriotism, 30
Peale, Norman Vincent, 117, 125, 132, 134–135, 137
Pecorini, Mr., 108
Pentecostalism, 14, 76, 151
Persecution
  Barone (Alfredo) experiencing, 3, 12, 22, 38–39, 85, 91–92
  of Italian Protestants, 39, 43–47, 88
Pirazzini, Agide, 20
Piscitelli, Domenico, 94
Pistrucci, Filippo, 55
Pius IX, Pope, 67, 74, 80
Pius X, Pope, 80
Politics and religion, 57–58, 77–80
  See also Catholic Church; Protestantism
Popes
  Leo XIII, 68
  Pius IX, 67, 74, 80
  Pius X, 80
  views on, 53, 74

Postethnic perspective, 132
The Power of Positive Thinking (Peale), 125
  See also Peale, Norman Vincent
Preaching styles, 135–136
Prior, Charles Edward, 141
Protestantism
  as ally of modernism, 81
  Anglo American Protestants, 79, 107–108, 145–146
  Catholic Church comparison, 90–91
  cooperation among churches, 100
  denominations of, 132–133, 151
  ex-priests as missionaries, 81
  geographic movement of missionaries, 141
  goodwill of, 70–71
  Italian identity and, 139–140
  for Italian immigrants, 97
  missionary obstacles, 141–142
  origins, 49–50
  struggling with Catholic Church, 39, 54–55, 92
  views on Catholic faith, 77–78
  See also Conversion to Protestantism; Italian Protestants; *specific denominations*
Protestant Missions to Catholic Immigrants (Abel), 28, 77
Protestant Witness (di Domenica), 35, 119
  See also di Domenica, Angelo
Public speaking, 135–136
Puzo, Mario, 17, 32–33, 34

Radicalism, 19–22
Rapisarda, Silvia, 146
Reason *vs.* emotional appeals, 117–119, 136
Religious colonialism, 39

Religious education in Italian schools, 147–148
Religious Work Among Italians in America (Mangano), 78, 81
Ricciardi, Natale, 61, 64, 110, 111–112
The Right Thing to Do (Hendin), 68–70
Risorgimento, 49–51, 54–55
 See also Garibaldi, Giuseppe; Unification of Italy
Roca, Antonio, 42, 100–101, 103
Roman Question, answers to
 Arrighi's writings, 71–74
 Belotti's writings, 70–71
 Catholic condemnation of modernism, 80–81
 di Donato's writings, 74–76
 Hendin's writings, 68–70
 Pentecostalism, 76
 Vesuvius eruption, 74
Rome in America (D'Agostino), 40
Rossetti, Gabriele, 55
Rubboli, Massimo, 2
Ruberto, Laura, 147
Ruddy, Anna, 17, 27–28

Saint Paul's Italian Episcopal Church (Hartford), 61, 100
Sannella, Francesco, 46–47, 59, 86, 96, 122–123
Sartorio, Enrico, 42, 47, 78, 95
Sbrocco, Pietro, 145–146
Science and religion, 55–56
Scripture. *See* Bible
Seale, Erwin, 130
Self-sacrifice, 21–22, 28
Settlement houses, 27–30
Sheldon, Charles, 35
Simple Steps (Caliandro), 133, 136, 137
Skinner, Lilian, 59

Socialism, 52
Social programs, 2, 27–30, 78, 110–112, 138
Son of Italy (D'Angelo), 11, 13
Sons of Italy (Mangano), 78
The Soul of an Immigrant (Panunzio), 22–23, 31
Southern and Northern Italy, comparison of, 60
Southern Baptists in Sunny Italy (Taylor), 97
The Southern Question (Gramsci), 52
South-North division of Italy, 52–57
Speranza, Gino, 17, 21, 77, 108
The Split-Level Trap (Gordon, Gordon, and Gunther), 125–126, 129–130
St. Paul's Italian Episcopal Church, 63, 110–111
St. Paul's Society, 29–30
State of Italy. *See* Unification of Italy
Statues of saints, 82
Stephenson, F. C., 78

Taylor, George Boardman, 39, 40, 42–43, 45, 92, 122
Taylor, George Braxton, 45–46, 91, 97
Tennent, Gilbert, 117–118, 136
Tent meetings, 119–120, 141–142
Terroni (Aprile), 50–51
Theology schools, 45, 123–124, 126–127
Thomas Hooker Club, 60–61
Tolino, John V., 78
Transformation as stage of religious work
 New Thought Movement, 128–130
 The Split-Level Trap and, 125–126
Tresca, Carlo, 52
Troward, Thomas, 127–128, 130
Turco, Lewis, 118–119, 127–128

Turco, Luigi, 8, 22–25, 33, 126–130, 137, 140, 146

Umbertina (Barolini), 17–18, 32, 34
Unification of Italy
  anti-Catholic sentiment and, 49–51
  Arrighi on, 71–74
  church-state conflict, 1
  differing views on, 55, 148
  North-South division, 52–57
  religion and, 40
  Risorgimento, 49–51, 54–55

Valdese Church (Rome), 1–2
Van Nest, Abraham Rynier, 113–114
Vasquez, Paolo, 29–30, 53, 61, 63, 64–65, 100, 110
Venturi, Robert, 148–149
Vesuvius eruption, 74

Village Street Mission, 107
Villari, Luigi, 52
Vizzini, Paul, 62
Vodola, Pietro, 111, 120

Wacker, Grant, 14
Walker, Robert (Roberto), 38, 39, 44, 86, 89–92
Ward, Michael T., 23
Wassef, Nadine, 148
Watt, Jon C., 29, 76
Whittinghill, D. G. (Dexter), 67, 122
Wilson, Tracey, 108
Women
  role of, 146–147
  as wives of Italian Protestant ministers, 145–146

Zito, William, 61–62, 69, 108